Edgar Klinger, Hans-Wolf Sievert, Günter Bierbrauer, Michael Harris Bond
Trust in German-Chinese Business Cooperation

Edgar Klinger, Hans-Wolf Sievert,
Günter Bierbrauer, Michael Harris Bond

Trust in German-Chinese Business Cooperation

Insights and Lessons to be Learned

DE GRUYTER

ISBN 978-3-11-134440-9
e-ISBN (PDF) 978-3-11-134456-0
e-ISBN (EPUB) 978-3-11-134460-7

Library of Congress Control Number: 2024932189

Bibliographic information published by the Deutsche Nationalbibliothek
The Deutsche Nationalbibliothek lists this publication in the Deutsche Nationalbibliografie;
detailed bibliographic data are available on the internet at http://dnb.dnb.de.

© 2024 Walter de Gruyter GmbH, Berlin/Boston
Cover image: Lingling Ni
Typesetting: Integra Software Services Pvt. Ltd.
Printing and binding: CPI books GmbH, Leck

www.degruyter.com

Acknowledgments

In recent years, it has become increasingly difficult to collect empirical data in China. This lamentable situation is due in particular to the reticence of Chinese individuals to participate in surveys and to provide information that may later prove to be "sensitive," especially when these data are provided to foreign scientists. Therefore, we are grateful to Dora Lau and especially Grace Poon, of The Chinese University of Hong Kong, who gave us significant support in preparing and conducting interviews with German and Chinese executives. The PricewaterhouseCoopers organization graciously supported us in finding suitable interview partners in China. We would like to thank Jörg Büechl for obtaining two Chinese native speakers who translated the interviews conducted in Putonghua into English. We also feel indebted to Helwig Schmidt-Glintzer, director of the China Centre at the University of Tübingen, who carefully reviewed the third chapter of this book and gave us valuable advice for its revision. We also feel obliged to thank Dr. Lingling Ni from the University of Göttingen for her valuable contributions.

We are grateful to Stefan Giesen, Jaya Dalal and Laura Booth from De Gruyter. Stefan Giesen trusted in our project and supervised it until completion. Jaya Dalal and Laura Booth provided invaluable support in overcoming several obstacles to complete the publication.

This study was granted funding from the Sievert Foundation for Science and Culture, Osnabrück. We are grateful to the foundation not only for the financial support, but also for the patience of its members, who had to wait longer than originally expected for the submission of the final report due to adverse general conditions for the implementation of the study during Covid.

While finishing this book the authors' memories are with Kwok Leung. He was a professor of management at the Chinese University of Hong Kong, his expertise was generally acknowledged in the field of Cross-Cultural Psychology and beyond. When we started to plan this research project, Professor Leung showed strong interest and promised his collaboration. A few days later he passed away unexpectedly. We acknowledge and praise his academic contributions to Cross-Cultural Psychology.

https://doi.org/10.1515/9783111344560-202

Contents

1 Introduction

For Germany, China is the second most important economic partner worldwide and the number one economic partner country in Asia. Furthermore, Germany is by far China's most important trading partner in considering the rest of Europe. According to the Federal Foreign Office, the bilateral trade volume in 2019 was approximately 206 billion Euros. German exports to China accounted for around 96 billion Euros and Chinese exports to Germany, approximately 110 billion Euros. The direct investment volume of German companies in China (including Hong Kong) was about 86.2 billion Euros in 2018. It has increased eightfold since 2000 (Dürr, Rammer & Böing, 2020). These statistics make China Germany's most important trading partner—ahead of the Netherlands and the USA.

The importance of the Chinese sales market may also be assessed by the sales and revenue shares of German companies achieved by the country in 2022. The German car manufacturers Volkswagen, BMW, Mercedes-Benz and Porsche each achieved from 30 to 40 percent of their sales in China. Merck, BASF and Siemens generate more than an eighth of their sales in China (Dostert et al., 2023).

For some time now, the supply relationships with China and their associated strategic interests have been increasingly called into question. In the recent past, the reason for this caution has been the Chinese government's handling of the corona pandemic and fears of growing tensions between China and the United States on the Taiwan issue. It is feared that there will be harsh reactions from the EU, and that the supply relationships could be disrupted (Busch, Mattes & Sultan, 2023). In addition, current media reports occasionally mention worries and fears about Germany's dependence on Chinese raw materials and finished products, as well as increasing discrimination against German companies in China. If one takes these reports on German–Chinese economic ties at face value, then the relationship between the two countries seems to be tense at the moment. Nevertheless, the investment plans of major German companies in China are larger than ever before (Dostert et al., 2023), even if the proportion of German companies operating in China planning future investments in the country is declining somewhat (Hildebrandt, Butek & Klose, 2022). Uncertainty mounts.

The changes in Chinese politics, economy and society that have been observed in recent years, and the reorientation of China policy by the political leadership of Germany and the EU determine the environment in which economic cooperation between German and Chinese companies have to navigate. In a recently published report, the German–Chinese Chamber of Commerce states that the backbones of the economic attractiveness of the Chinese market, which have persuaded many foreign companies to do business in China in recent decades, have lost their viability. "The Old China Story" may come to an end (Butek et al., 2023). With a reference to the Chinese proverb,

https://doi.org/10.1515/9783111344560-001

> *When the winds of change blow, some build walls, but others build windmills.*
> (当改革之风吹起之时, 有人筑墙抵抗, 有人顺势造风车。)

the report of the Chamber of Foreign Trade formulates the expectation that multinational companies can continue to be successful in China by adjusting their business activities in China. Hope persists.

Until 2001, a foreign company's decision to do business in China almost inevitably meant that it would set up a joint venture with a Chinese company. In the 1980s, approximately 90 percent of foreign investors' involvement in China was in the form of joint ventures. Thirty years later, about every eighth engagement in China was a joint venture with a Chinese cooperation partner (Vollmer, 2012). Since 2018, the obligation to establish a joint venture, which previously applied to several branches of industry, has been gradually lifted. However, this relaxation of requirement will not result in joint ventures being completely phased out for investments in China (Stepan-Meyer, 2021).

Since January 1, 2020, the Foreign Investment Law (FIL) of the People's Republic of China has come into force. From that moment, a uniform law for all forms of investment has been promulgated to apply throughout the country for the first time. The new law repealed the existing laws on equity joint ventures, contractual joint ventures and wholly foreign-owned enterprises, along with their respective implementing regulations.

What makes international joint ventures successful? Key success factors include the strategic fit of the partner company, the material and political-relational incentives associated with founding the joint venture and the cultural compatibility of the joint venture partners. However, the role of one factor in the successful establishment and management of joint ventures has remained a desideratum in previous research: the mutual trust of the managers involved.

The question of the mutual trust between German and Chinese executives who work in joint ventures is in the focus of the present study. Chinese and European executives' assessments and judgements about their mutual trust will be revealed through a series of guided interviews. Detailed reference will be made to the cultural differences between the two countries, to the worldviews characterizing China and Germany and their impact on the behavior of executives when working with executives of European origin. Recommendations for action are derived from the interviews, which may contribute to more successful cooperation in German–Chinese business cooperation, but also help to build better understanding among Chinese and German partners in establishing future joint enterprises.

Structure of the Book

In Chapters 2 and 3 we address the institutional, cultural and religious-ideological framework conditions under which trust is formed between executives of European and Chinese origin at German–Chinese joint ventures located in China. First, the nature and objectives of international joint ventures are explained in the second chapter. In addition, an overview of findings on the success factors of such joint ventures is given. This review shows that the handling and overcoming of the cultural differences of all managers involved as well as the successful development of mutual trust are among the key success factors. Therefore, a presentation of several concepts describing and structuring these cultural differences follows. Based on these concepts, the cultural similarities and differences between the national cultures of Germany and China are outlined. Furthermore, the central concept of interpersonal trust is specified from both a Western European and from a Chinese perspective. In the third chapter, Confucianism, Daoism and Buddhism are explained as the religious and ideological currents that have significantly influenced the cultural orientations found in China today.

The focus of this book is the documentation of an empirical study aimed at gaining insights into the mutual trust of the managers involved in the management of joint ventures. A qualitative approach is followed: Managers with experience in German–Chinese business cooperation were asked to report on their assessments and experiences in semi-structured interviews. The interview guidelines used for this purpose follow a theoretically sound framework that is presented in the fourth chapter. Information on the procedure for data collection and data analysis is given in the fifth chapter.

In the sixth chapter, results are presented along with the previously developed theoretical framework for interpersonal trust. Here, relevant quotes from the interviews are presented that reveal similarities and differences in the mutual trust of the managers.

In the seventh chapter, we provide recommendations for action derived from these previously documented results. Careful consideration should contribute to building mutual trust in German–Chinese business cooperation.

2 Fundamentals

Joint Ventures as a Market Entry Strategy

The global economic recovery after the end of the Second World War led to a rapidly expanding economic integration and interdependence across countries and continents. New internationalization theories and market entry strategies emerged. The newer forms of market entry also include international joint ventures (IJVs), which not only Bleicher and Hermann (1991, p. 5) consider to be a "fascinating form of entrepreneurial activity." Although the number of IJVs in China is currently declining (China Statistical Yearbook, 2015–2020 editions), this type of joint venture is still common among newly established companies.

But why are IJVs such an appealing form of market entry? For many companies, this form of market entry is more advantageous than alternative options of market entry (e.g., founding a 100 percent subsidiary, import–export or license agreements) for several reasons that will be outlined in this chapter. Joint venture management is also an attractive field of research. This is indicated by the large number of publications on this subject. Nippa and Reuer (2019) report that, meanwhile, there are more than 800 publications about joint venture management. Understandably, the field of intercultural management, which deals with the influence of culture on economic activities, has received new impetus through the growing number of joint ventures established: People from different cultures working together in one company, quite frequently in the form of a joint venture, became a much noticed and highly relevant research area (Sievert, 2009).

Joint ventures as a form of market entry are closely linked to the economic history of modern China. It denotes the transition from the socialist planned economy under Mao Zedong (1893–1976) to the socialist market economy under Deng Xiao Ping (1904–1997). The central objectives of Mao's policy included striving for self-sufficiency, the implementation of a planned economy and the realization of social equality. For example, members of the military did not wear any insignia of rank at this time. The campaigns initiated by Mao—such as the "Great Leap Forward," "Let a Thousand Flowers Bloom" and the "Cultural Revolution"—led to the decline of the Chinese economy and plunged the country into abysmal social chaos.

Mao's revolutionary excesses claimed tens of millions of lives (Branigan, 2023). In a society where denouncing parents was declared a revolutionary act, interpersonal trust was destroyed. Whether and to what extent this fundamental social capital has since been restored is a matter of lively debate (Linggi, 2011). The current Chinese government is working towards raising and stabilizing the level of trust that exists at the societal and individual levels. For this purpose, a regulatory system has been established, which is described as the so-called "social credit system" (社会信用体系) (Gesk, 2020). The aim is to create more security and order and thus more trust

https://doi.org/10.1515/9783111344560-002

through a digital surveillance system. Similar systems of social control have always existed in Chinese history (Schmidt-Glintzer, 2020). It will be interesting to see how the social credit system experiment will develop and whether this latest strategy will succeed in restoring the trust that was damaged in the course of Mao's revolutionary efforts.

Deng Xiao Ping, Mao's true successor, was free from the revolutionary pathos of his predecessor. Unlike the Great Helmsman Mao, Deng was pragmatic; as his oft-quoted pronouncement asserts: "It doesn't matter whether a cat is black or white, [the main thing is that] it catches mice" (Li, 1977). Deng's aim was to lift the ailing economy and to lead the Chinese people living in great abject poverty out of economic and social misery. As one of his first measures, he gave the population the opportunity to earn money individually in agriculture and industry. "Enrich yourself!": That was the motto he called out to his fellow citizens in 1978, most of whom lived at the poverty line (Fargel, 2014). With the encouragement provided by the Self-Responsibility System to enrich oneself, Deng set in motion a dynamic that continues to this day. The high growth rates of the Chinese economy over many years have their origin here.

Another reason for China's economic boom that persisted for some 30-years is that Deng Xiao Ping abolished his predecessor's self-reliance policy for China and instead initiated an open-door policy (开放政策). A key element of this policy was inviting foreign companies to enter the Chinese market and invest in the country. Industrial companies from abroad were invited to transfer their know-how to the Middle Kingdom and thereby contribute to the reconstruction and renewal of the Chinese economy. However, Deng imposed one condition for foreign companies interested in entering the Chinese market: The entry into the promising Chinese market was only possible by founding a joint venture with a Chinese partner company. In the 1990s, the local cooperation partner had to be granted a capital share of at least 50 percent. This obligation to involve a domestic joint venture partner was removed for most industries when China joined the World Trade Organization (WTO) in 2001.

What is a Joint Venture?

The market entry form of a joint venture is a legally independent organization established by (usually two) independent companies and managed jointly by the parent companies. Joint ventures may take many forms. Joint ventures can be founded in order to implement cooperation in the areas of production, sales or research and development. Most joint ventures are organized across functions. In addition, a distinction can be made between joint ventures that are predominantly in one country and those that operate internationally. "International joint ventures" are those joint ventures in which at least one of the joint venture partners is not domiciled in the country in which the joint venture has its official headquarters (Eisele, 1995).

An empirically based theory of joint ventures has not yet been developed. In the theoretical clarification of joint venture-specific issues, the findings of transaction cost theory, organizational theory, contingency theory, and theories of strategic management are used (Hornung, 2013; Rohm, 2017). Meanwhile, research results exist for several areas of joint venture management, for instance, on the objectives of joint venture formations. Based on Bleicher and Hermann (1991) and Eisele (1995), these can be summarized as follows:

- Synergy effects: Effects that result from the purposeful cooperation of the joint venture partners. For example, the bundling of production capacities may lead to a more efficient use of resources and thus to an increase in corporate profitability.
- Furthermore, access to the resources and markets required for joint activities can be facilitated by forming a joint venture, according to the motto, "We provide the know-how, the partner the know-who."
- In addition, joint ventures are a popular means of protecting against risks, because none of the partners has to bear the entire entrepreneurial risk alone.
- Joint ventures can also be used to implement governmental objectives, such as in China in the era of Deng Xiao Ping. Deng hoped that the technology transfer organized by founding joint ventures would boost the modernization of the Chinese economy.

However, establishing a joint venture can also have disadvantages: the partner companies involved in a joint venture are limited both in their decision-making power and their power of disposition; they must, therefore, coordinate with their partner. For this reason, many foreign investors now prefer to set up 100 percent subsidiaries in China, since this market entry strategy has been legal there since 2001. Product piracy represents another danger for joint venture management. In the first few years of the "open door policy" the theft of intellectual property with respect to the technological resources brought into a joint venture was acquisitively pursued under the supervision of the state. Many foreign investors found that the technical know-how they introduced in China was "transferred" to their partner's company and then used in competition with the joint venture. The *Herald Tribune* (October 10, 2005) vividly summarized the economic effect of such a know-how transfer:

> *The highly impressive development of the Chinese economy is largely based on the theft of intellectual property.*

More recently, know-how transfer is better protected by law in China. It is still a key factor, however, de-motivating the establishment of joint ventures.

Success Factors of International Joint Ventures

The search for success factors has become one of the central areas in joint venture research. This applies especially to China with its particularly difficult economic environment for foreign investors (Wuttke, 2012; Butek et al., 2023). Identifying the determinants of joint venture success is therefore addressed in most publications dealing with the development of joint ventures in China.

Among the pioneers of German joint venture research were the already-mentioned authors, Bleicher and Hermann (1991), who were especially interested in identifying the success factors in the management of joint ventures. However, they did not specifically address the Chinese market. In their work, a total of seven determinants are listed as key success factors of joint ventures. These include the promoters of a joint venture, the strategic fit, the cultural sympathy of the joint venture partners, the incentives associated with founding a joint venture, the legal framework, the negotiating positions of the partners and the arrangements for the dissolution of a joint venture. However, the factors presented by Bleicher and Hermann are not weighed among each other and are not empirically verified.

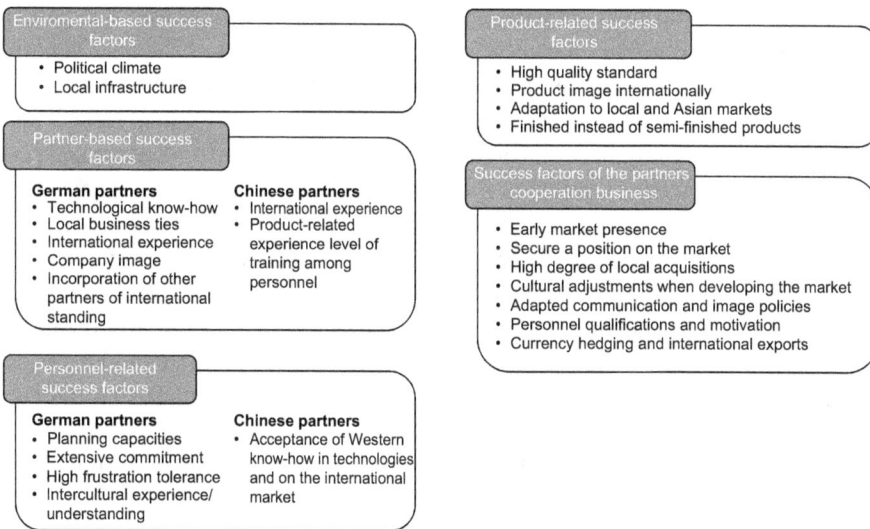

Enviromental-based success factors
- Political climate
- Local infrastructure

Partner-based success factors

German partners	Chinese partners
• Technological know-how	• International experience
• Local business ties	• Product-related
• International experience	experience level of
• Company image	training among
• Incorporation of other	personnel
partners of international	
standing	

Personnel-related success factors

German partners	Chinese partners
• Planning capacities	• Acceptance of Western
• Extensive commitment	know-how in technologies
• High frustration tolerance	and on the international
• Intercultural experience/	market
understanding	

Product-related success factors
- High quality standard
- Product image internationally
- Adaptation to local and Asian markets
- Finished instead of semi-finished products

Success factors of the partners cooperation business
- Early market presence
- Secure a position on the market
- High degree of local acquisitions
- Cultural adjustments when developing the market
- Adapted communication and image policies
- Personnel qualifications and motivation
- Currency hedging and international exports

Figure 2.1: Success factors of Sino-German joint ventures from the perspective of German managers (adapted from Trommsdorff & Wilpert, 1994).

Trust as a Success Factor of Joint Ventures?

Neither in Trommsdorff and Wilpert (1994; see Figure 2.1) nor in other publications presented in the 1990s (Peill-Schoeller, 1994; Schuchardt, 1994; Chung & Sievert, 1995;

Büchel et al., 1997) was trust mentioned as a success factor of joint ventures. Depending on the question and the scientific position of the author, various determinants of business success were identified in these studies. What all have in common is that the success factors are seen as rather independent determinants of the success of joint ventures.

None of these studies includes an in-depth scientific examination of the phenomenon of trust as a success factor in joint venture management. Only Büchel et al. (1997, p. 171) briefly mention trust as a "basic factor of joint venture management." In the German-speaking regions, the connections between trust and joint venture management have not been discussed to date—in contrast to the Anglo-American-speaking regions, where research on this topic has been reported since the 1990s. Among others, the studies of Madhok (1995) should be mentioned here because he is one of the pioneers of American joint venture research. For Madhok, a joint venture is a social entity constituted by the interactions of individual employees. He defines a joint venture as a "mixture of both contract and commitment. This commitment develops through interaction and results in a trust-based relationship" (Madhok, 1995, p. 25).

The dynamics of a joint venture are determined by the interaction of two different but related objectives: Both the output and performance of the joint venture must correspond to the business objectives and agreements of the partner companies ("structural mechanisms" or "contracts"). Management processes of the joint venture must ensure successful collaboration in the joint venture ("social mechanisms"). These structural and social mechanisms become effective through interactions and are the basis for ongoing trustful cooperation in the company. Interpersonal trust among company employees grows to the extent that the joint venture management succeeds in realizing these socio-structural objectives.

According to Madhok (1995), successful joint venture management predominantly requires paying attention to the social dimension. The one-sided focus on costs and returns, which is repeatedly noticeable in the management of joint ventures (Beamish & Banks, 1987), leads to reduced motivation and dissatisfaction among employees. This narrow focus impairs the company's performance: "Sole emphasis on the outcome neglects the social context within which the relationship is embedded" (Madhok, 1995, p. 5). According to Madhok, this is where the frequent failure of joint ventures arises. With this insight, his approach represents a further contribution to the topic of "success factors of joint ventures."

The research by Ng, Lau and Nyaw (2007) also emphasizes the connections between trust and joint venture success. They focus on the importance of trust between the joint venture partners as a factor in their success. The trust between the joint venture partners (i.e., between the parent companies) represents a special form of trust that has so far received little attention in research. According to Ng et al. (2007, p. 431) this form of trust ranks among the key success factors of joint venture management: "Trust between partners is suggested to be an important factor that contributes to the success of IJV."

Ng et al. (2007) investigated the causal relationships between the success of the joint venture and the trust between the joint venture partners as part of a study of IJVs in China. The positive effects that the trust among the joint venture partners has on the company's success are shown for selected subject areas. The subject areas addressed in this study include entering the local market, intercultural distance and the particular challenges faced by management.

The advantageous effects of a trustful cooperation among joint venture partners can have an effect as early as the market entry phase. The establishment of the company in a market (in this phase usually the local market) generally runs much more smoothly if the joint venture partners trust each other and actively support the management in market development, procurement and sales. Distrust among the joint venture partners can significantly affect the initial growth phase, because in this case there is a risk that the frictions among the partners will be transmitted down to the management level.

According to Ng et al. (2007), a similarly crucial challenge is overcoming the joint partners' intercultural distance. The success of a joint venture depends to a large extent on the fact that the representatives of the different cultural groups in the company cooperate successfully despite the cultural differences between them. This consideration also applies at the level of the joint venture partners. The decisions made in the management teams of the joint venture partners control the fate and thus the success of the company in the long term. They can only be brought about if there is mutual trust among these partners.

The leadership expertise of the management should also be considered in this context. According to Ng et al. (2007), the well-being of a joint venture depends to a large extent on the leadership skills of the managers of the joint venture. This consideration applies in particular to the general manager of the IJV, since he or she embodies the central link between the parent or partner companies and the joint venture. In this role, his or her responsibilities not only include cultivating relationships with the representatives of the joint venture partners, but also involving them in the IJV's corporate decision-making processes for important deals. Decision-making will be easier if the cooperation between the joint venture partners is based on mutual trust. If, on the other hand, the general manager has to mediate and compensate between the partners, this intervention might tie up his or her energies that could be better used for other managerial tasks.

Surveying the issues arising from the findings of the Ng et al. (2007) study emphasizes the conclusion that in joint venture management, trust between the joint venture partners is a success factor that should not be overlooked.

Similar to the phenomenon of trust, the factor of culture played a subordinate role in joint venture research for a long time. In the study by Trommsdorff and Wilpert (1994 p. 73) mentioned above, "intercultural understanding" is only briefly mentioned as one of many personal success factors, but culture as a success factor is not further discussed. This missing consideration also applies to most of the studies published in the 1990s. This view has survived up until now, as is illustrated by an empirical study on what is probably the most famous and most successful of all German–Chinese joint ventures, the joint venture between SAIC and Volkswagen in Shanghai (Gewiss & Oestersporkmann, 2017). Here, too, the culture factor is regarded as just one among many determinants of joint venture success (see Figure 2.2).

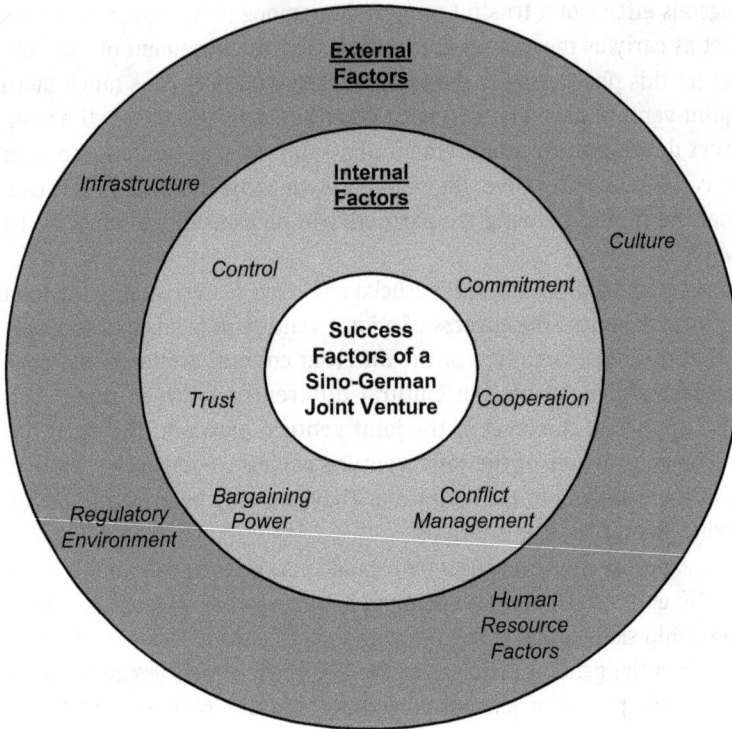

Figure 2.2: Success factors of the German–Chinese joint venture between SAIC und Volkswagen (adapted from Gewiss & Oestersporkmann, 2017).

The monography on joint venture management presented by Eisele in 1995 represents a significant expansion of the research spectrum. In his study, he examines the entrepreneurial phases of initiation, negotiation and implementation within the framework of a so-called transaction episodes approach regarding their contribution to the success of a joint venture. The choice of a partner in the initiation phase, the development of trust in the negotiation phase and the joint development of the company organization in the implementation phase have—alongside other determinants—proven to be critical to success. Because the individual joint venture phases are interconnected, the phase-specific determinants are also part of an interconnected system of success factors. With this approach, Eisele (1995) deviates from the isolated presentation of individual success factors. Rather, he sees them as interwoven determinants geared towards entrepreneurial success. However, Eisele (1995) also missed the opportunity to take an intercultural perspective and thus failed to present a more detailed examination of culture as a success factor.

Lang's (1998) empirical study on intercultural management in China focuses on the intercultural aspect. The author analyzes joint ventures from the perspective of intercultural management. Central to his work is an analysis of how cultural differences shape and influence the behavior of managers and about the ways of bridging these differences. He examines the extent to which the values, attitudes and behavior of the managers of international joint ventures whose managers he interviewed (Europeans, Chinese and Japanese) are shaped by their respective cultures of origin and how the resulting cultural differences can be bridged through targeted intercultural management.

Lang examines this with regard to five research areas: corporate environment, organizational and cooperation patterns, management processes, attitude towards work, and interpersonal relationships. According to Lang (1998), an international joint venture can only succeed if the employees are successfully integrated into the company, irrespective of their different cultural backgrounds. Here, the company management is required to develop a cross-cultural common understanding of the company through intercultural empathy and bonding ("Developing a common understanding of the firm," Lang, 1998, p. 282). According to Lang, bridging the intercultural differences found in a company (IMD – Intercultural Management Differences) is one of the key success factors. However, the individual IMDs are not weighted. Likewise, the causal relationships between the individual determinants are not examined.

In her empirical study of Austrian–Chinese joint ventures, Salomon (2008) also deals intensively with the problem of identifying success factors. Her findings go well beyond what previous joint venture studies have produced. This applies above all to the culture factor. Salomon distinguishes much more clearly than her predecessors between soft (essentially cultural) and hard (i.e., essentially environmental) determinants of success. After a thorough evaluation of her data, she concludes that soft and hard success factors are of similar importance for joint ventures. The success factor most frequently mentioned by the international managers surveyed by Salomon (2008) is intercultural understanding. This factor involves the ability to accept, understand and respect partners and their culture. Remember, in the study by Trommsdorff and Wilpert (1994), intercultural understanding was but one of several residual variables.

Intermediate Result

In joint venture research, much greater importance has been attached to the factors of culture and trust in the recent past. This insight should be made more prominent among managers: Among those who are involved in international business the cultural aspect of corporate management does not seem to be given the attention it deserves (Sievert, Klinger & Bierbrauer, 2010). The same applies to the trust factor.

If the relatively short period of time since the beginning of research into joint ventures is taken into consideration, the large number of publications on this topic is remarkable. Nevertheless, many questions remain unanswered, which future research will have to answer (Nippa & Reuer, 2019). This includes, above all, the question of the conditions under which the cultures working together in an international joint venture come together and develop into a new and viable "interculture" (Mauritz, 1996, p. 98). The growing knowledge about the interrelationships between joint ventures and culture will show the possibilities and ways with which the management of intercultural joint ventures can be further improved.

What is Trust?

As already mentioned, trust is one of the key factors for the success of international joint ventures. This construct is in the focus of our study. Trust is an expression that is frequently used in everyday language. It characterizes a specific form of relationship. In everyday life, we often come across statements that people trust their doctor as well as their parents, they trust advertising claims as well as their automobile, they trust politicians and their electricity supplier, a nuclear power plant or the safety equipment of a cable car that they are about to enter. Whenever people talk about trust, an object reference can be observed: the trust is in another person, a system, a device or a technology, a company, a rule, or a statement, etc. DeSteno (2014) points out that we can or must also trust ourselves, for example, when it comes to behaving in a future challenging situation (examination, coping with a complex leadership problem). This denotes what we expect of ourselves or what others hope they can expect of us.

The German word "Vertrauen" developed from the Old High German "fertruen" and goes back to the Gothic word "trauan." It belongs to the word group that includes being faithful, having courage, hope and belief. The English word "trust" is consistent with these meanings.

In the Western tradition, influenced by Judeo-Christian religion, the sacrifice of Isaac is probably the oldest and most well-known narrative about trust. It is found in the Old Testament of the Bible. According to this story, God commands Abraham to sacrifice his son Isaac in order to test Abraham's willingness to obey God, that is, his trust in God. Abraham was ready to carry out God's command. At the last moment, just before Abraham was about to stab his son, an angel from God intervened and stopped Abraham, declaring that God only wanted to test Abraham's faith. Abraham's motives can be seen as a mixture of obedience in God, courage to commit homicide and a willingness to take risks. His motives are based on trust in God. He was willing to place his son's life in the hands of God, trusting in God's wisdom and care, and the hope of eternal life. Abraham's trust is future-oriented and is associated with the risk of failure that could have consisted in God's changing His mind in His all-encompassing power and wisdom.

If an expression is widely used in everyday language, it is not uncommon for conceptual imprecisions to arise. In a broad, philosophically oriented analysis, Hartmann (2020) examines the question of whether there is a growing crisis of trust in our society. He concludes that there can hardly be any talk of a crisis of trust because many alleged crises relate less to trust. This finding illustrates the requirement that a scientific discussion of a phenomenon that is of considerable everyday relevance must precisely outline what is meant.

Trust is an object of psychological or sociological, economic, or philosophical studies and research—to name just a few of the disciplines involved. From the perspectives of the various scientific disciplines, different aspects of what is meant by trust are focused in both theoretical discussions and empirical research studies. This conceptual diversity exacerbates the exchange of information across disciplines and complicates the integration of research findings on trust.

Since the 1980s, the variety and lack of precision in definitions of trust have repeatedly been deplored (e.g., Lewis & Weigert, 1985; Shapiro, 1987; Taylor, 1989; Wrightsman, 1991; Lewicki & Bunker, 1995). In theoretical reflections on trust, and even more so in the operationalization of trust measures, it often remains unclear whether determinants of trust, components of trust or consequences of trust are being considered (Mayer, Davis & Schoorman, 1995; McKnight, Cummings & Chervany, 1998). In contrast to trust, dependability means a property of people, but, e.g., also of systems or processes, which describes the extent to which people's actions occur in accordance with the expectations of observers or persons party to the interaction. These expectations relate to the compliance of a person's behavior with the rules, which can be demonstrated by compliance with the law, social norms or self-imposed patterns of action.

In one example, Hartmann (2020) refers to the reliability of Immanuel Kant, who set out for a walk through Königsberg every day at a certain time of day—i.e., reliably. This example illustrates a key difference between trust and reliability. Trust means that the trustor expects a benefit from the behavior of the trustee. However, such an expectation of benefit does not exist in the case of reliability. Reliability is a requirement typically placed on systems and processes. Systems and processes do not bring any added benefit, but "only" have to function as specified by their design and by technical settings.

Regarding the object of trust, a distinction is often made between personal trust and system trust (Giddens, 1999; Luhmann, 2014). Personal trust is directed towards individuals with whom the trustor is in contact and with whom they may interact in the foreseeable future. Personal trust refers either to this specific interaction person(s) (= interpersonal trust) or to the basic willingness to trust one's fellow human beings (= generalized or dispositional trust) (Rotter, 1967). System trust stands for the expectation that within a certain system (e.g., a nation state, a company, an organization or authority) principles apply. It is assumed that these principles are adhered to and that, therefore, the functionality of the system is maintained (Giddens, 1999). Gilbert (2010, pp. 171–172) emphasizes that actors "are inevitably dependent on a sufficient degree of trust in the system for successful economic transactions to occur."

However, the concept of system trust understood in this way clearly reveals the vagueness of the concept of trust: In systems, the actors can reliably follow principles and take them into account and comply with them in their transactions. The result shows the reliability of the system. According to the concept of trust represented here, one cannot speak of trust in this case, because a system in itself cannot act benevolently, but at best can function in accordance with the rules and thus proceed neutrally. In this respect, it is better to speak of perceived system reliability than of trust in the system. For our subsequent considerations, the focus will be on personal and interpersonal trust.

Trust always plays a role when the consequences of one's own activities also depend on the actions of at least one other actor. In this situation, trust stands for the expectation that the other actor (= trustee) will behave in such a way that the trustor will benefit from the trustee's actions. The trustor thus becomes dependent on the trustee. This constellation is often described as vulnerability. Thus, Mayer, Davis and Schoorman (1995, p. 712) define trust in this sense as "the willingness of a party to be vulnerable to the actions of another party based on the expectation that the other will perform a particular action important to the trustor, irrespective of the ability to monitor or control that other party." The aspect of vulnerability can also be found in a definition proposed by Rousseau et al. (1998, p. 395): "Trust is a psychological state comprising the intention to accept vulnerability based upon positive expectations of the intentions or behavior of another." If one takes these quoted definitions of trust as a basis, then (1) uncertainty (2) in a situation of outcome dependency can be recognized as the essential framework conditions of psychological, sociological and economic concepts of interpersonal trust. A positive correlation is usually assumed between perceived insecurity and trust (e.g., Koller, 1988).

With their conception of the trust construct, Rousseau et al. (1998, p. 395) go a decisive step further: "Trust is not a behavior (e.g., cooperation), or a choice (e.g., taking a risk), but an underlying psychological condition that can cause or result from such actions." Thus, Rousseau et al. introduce the idea of a credit account for trust: a minimum level of trust in the prospective cooperation partner is a prerequisite for the initiation of a cooperation in a situation of uncertainty. As the cooperation progresses, the actors keep gaining new samples of the trustworthiness of the respective partner. They will then increase their trust in the partner in the case of positive results or reduce it in the case of results that fall short of expectations and for which the partner is blamed. In some situations, their trust in their partner may not change (e.g., Larson, 1992; Ring & van de Ven, 1994; Boersma, Buckley & Ghauri, 2003). This process can also be described as the dynamic of trust, which, if positive, leads to a reduction in complexity (Luhmann, 2014). Trust is thus an expression of growing confidence in being able to predict the positive intentions of an interaction partner.

What Does Trust Induce?

After providing a theoretical specification of the construct of trust, we next consider the question of the effects of personal trust. Here the question of the economic consequences is paramount.

Dirks and Ferrin (2001) have prepared the ground for an extensive literature analysis conducted by Gilbert (2010). He presents the results of numerous empirical studies in which significant effects of trust on economically relevant variables are reported. The effects of trust that reduce the transaction costs of companies are reported frequently (e.g., Arrow, 1972; Bromiley & Cummings, 1995; Currall & Judge, 1995; Zaheer, McEvily & Perrone, 1998; Bartelt, 2002; Davis et al., 2000). Luhmann (2014) also focuses on reducing complexity and its consequences for transaction costs. Likewise, frequently positive effects of trust on the performance of companies and company cooperations have been found (e.g., Oldham, 1975; Rich, 1997; Dirks, 2000; Kale, Singh & Perlmutter, 2000; Morrow Jr., Hansen & Pearson, 2004). The establishment of business cooperation is also facilitated by mutual trust (e.g., Nooteboom, Berger & Noorderhaven, 1997; Kale, Singh & Perlmutter, 2000; Eggs, 2001; Clases, Bachmann & Wehner, 2004). Moreover, there are numerous empirical studies on the effects of trust on individual cognitive and affective determinants of the economic success of various forms of entrepreneurial cooperation, as Gilbert's (2010) overview shows.

These findings on the effects of individual personal trust are supplemented by macroeconomic studies of the effects of different general trust in societies. A study by Zak and Knack (2001) shows that a lack of trust in a society can be compensated for by setting up institutions to monitor and control transactions, which serve to check the trustworthiness of economic actors. The social credit system (社会信用体系) currently emerging in the People's Republic of China may serve this purpose (Gesk, 2020).

Zaheer, McEvily, and Perrone (1998, p. 142) distinguish between (1) interpersonal trust "as the extent of a boundary-spanning agent's trust in her counterpart in the [partner] organization" and (2) interorganizational trust "as the extent of trust placed in the partner organization by the members of a focal organization." Both trust concepts differentiated by Zaheer et al. are understood as coherent and have an impact on the results of the cooperation between the partner organizations. In the course of their theoretical considerations, Currall and Inkpen (2002) conclude that when organizations work together, there is trust on the (1) individual, interpersonal level, on the (2) intergroup level or on the (3) interorganizational level. The considerations of Zaheer, McEvily and Perrone (1998) and of Currall and Inkpen (2002) agree that trust is not only understood as an interpersonal phenomenon. Rather, the people within an organization, e.g., employees of a JV partner company, can have a more or less trusting collective relationship with another organization, e.g., the other JV partner company or companies. Both interpersonal and intergroup trust can have a significant impact on the relationships between the organizations involved in a joint venture.

Even after some 50 years of empirical trust research in psychology, sociology, economics and other scientific disciplines, there are inconsistent ideas about the dimensionality of trust. These are often based on the conception of trust as a context-specific construct (e.g., Rousseau et al., 1998; Hardin, 2002). In their extensive inventory of empirical studies on interpersonal trust within organizations, McEvily and Tortoriello (2011, p. 33) arrive at the judgment that trust should be understood as a multidimensional construct and state: "Given its complexity, in many circumstances it would seem appropriate to operationalize trust as a multi-dimensional construct and empirically assess the extent to which distinct dimensions exist and the nature and degree of their relationship to each other." In about 78 percent of 207 relevant empirical studies, interpersonal trust was operationalized uni-dimensionally; multidimensional operationalizations were used in the remaining studies. Integrity, ability, benevolence and affective trust were used most frequently as trust dimensions (McEvily & Tortoriello, 2011). The first three dimensions mentioned can be summarized as cognitive trust, as is particularly the case with the framework suggested by Mayer, Davis and Schoorman (1995; see also Mayer & Davis, 1999).

Interorganizational Trust-Building Processes

As possible foundations for interorganizational trust, Child, Faulkner and Tallman (2005) consider the existence of a clear cost–benefit calculation, the development of a mutual understanding of the problems and challenges of the respective partner company and the development of relationships or even friendships between the individuals involved. Furthermore, the reputation of a company as a reliable player is also an important prerequisite for initiating cooperation. Referring to three perspectives of trust proposed by Lane (1998), they differentiate between three phases in the development of interorganizational trust:

- Calculative trust, where "trusting involves expectations about another, based on calculations which weigh the costs and benefits of certain courses of action to either the trustor or the trustee" (Lane, 1998, p. 5). This form of trust is likely to be particularly important for the start-up phase of business partnerships. For example, if two companies agree to set up a joint venture despite significant perceived risks, trust will primarily be based on such a calculation.
- Knowledge-based trust: The mutual knowledge gained from experience about the respective partner company, which increases across the course of cooperating, expands the basis for a trusting cooperation. Across the course of continued cooperation, the cooperating organizations and their actors learn to understand one

another and may even be able to successfully predict the reasoning and actions of the actors in the partner company. This form of trust is also based on the exchange of knowledge and on the common ways of reasoning that develop during the process. In addition, mutual understanding and any congruence of goals that may result are further bases for trust (Lane, 1998).
–   Identification-based trust: A prerequisite for this form of trust is that the actors share common values and a common concept of moral obligation. In the course of working together, friendships can develop because of this emerging sense of commonality. The resulting emotional bonds then form the basis for identification-based trust.

Trust in International Business Relations

International economic relations transcend the boundaries of cultural and institutional systems. In addition to the difficulties in economic relationships within the same system, they therefore pose a particular challenge for building trust (Parkhe, 1993; Child, Faulkner and Tallman, 2005), as Zaheer and Zaheer (2006, p. 21) also emphasize: "Not only do the levels and degree of trust differ across international borders, but also the very nature of trust can vary in different national contexts." Similarly, Doney, Cannon and Mullen (1998, p. 607) posit: "[Since] societal norms and values that establish 'appropriate' beliefs and behavioral standards tend to vary across cultures, the processes trustors use to form trust may depend heavily on culture." In addition, there is the challenge associated with an equivalent translation of operationalizations of individual trust dimensions into different languages (McEvily & Tortoriello, 2011). Zaheer and Zaheer (2006, p. 22) conclude: "By ignoring the institutional and cultural embeddedness of trust in different national contexts, [trust] research may be reaching erroneous conclusions."

Up until the mid-2010s, there were very few empirical studies on differences in trust between actors with different cultural orientations who established cooperative relationships. The types of relationships examined, and the cultural orientations of the people involved, differed. The cultural orientations were most frequently operationalized by cultural differences measured in different ways (e.g., Aulakh, Kotabe & Sahay, 1996; Luo, 2001; Huff & Kelley, 2003; Stahl, Chua & Pablo, 2003). Doney, Cannon and Mullen (1998) offered 15 hypotheses to describe the relationship between cultural orientations and trust-building processes. In their reasoning, they refer to four cultural dimensions described by Hofstede (1980). In their model of trust-building, the authors differentiate between cognitive and non-cognitive processes, but the formation of hypotheses is limited to cognitive processes. When modeling trust, the authors use the framework suggested by Mayer, Davis and Schoorman (1995) and distinguish between five processes (calculative, prediction, intentionality, capability, transference) of cognitive trust-building (Doney, Cannon and Mullen, 1998). However, processes of trust-building in relationships between people or groups with different cultural orientations are not considered in their work. For situations of inconsistency in the cultural orientations of actors, Doney, Cannon and Mullen (1998, p. 617) simply state: "A lack of congruence in cultural proclivities may result in a virtual collapse of the trust-building mechanism."

Cultural Orientations from a Western Perspective

The work of Doney, Cannon and Mullen (1998) draws attention to concepts for describing and explaining cultural differences. Western academics from various disciplines have presented models and measurements of concepts that differ more or less clearly in terms of the underlying definitions of culture, the theoretical foundations, their empirical validation and their proposed operationalizations (cf. the overview in Müller & Gelbrich, 2015). Since the concept of culture is used in a variety of ways both in the academic field and in everyday life, a basic definition should be found for a clearer understanding of what is meant by culture.

Tylor (1871, p. 1) was most probably the first social scientist who tried to define the concept of culture: "Culture is that complex whole which includes knowledge, belief, art, morals, law, custom, and any other capabilities and habits acquired by a man as a member of society." Perhaps the most commonly used definition was proposed by Herskovits in the 1940s. According to him, culture is "the man-made part of the human environment" (Herskovits, 1948, p. 17). The US-American organizational psychologist Schein suggested the following definition: "The culture of a group can be defined as a pattern of shared basic assumptions that the group learned as it solved its problems of external adaptation and internal integration, that has worked well enough to be considered valid and, therefore, to be taught to new members as the correct way to perceive, think, and feel in relation to those problems" (Schein, 1992, p. 12).

More recent definitions show striking parallels to Tylor's definition of culture. David Thomas and Mark Peterson (2018, p. 24) propose the following definition: "Culture is a set of knowledge structures consisting of systems of values, norms, attitudes, beliefs, and behavioral meanings that are shared by members of a social group (society) and embedded in its institutions and that are learned from previous generations." Similarly, House and Javidan (2004, p. 15) define culture: "as shared motives, values, beliefs, identities, and interpretations or meanings of significant events that result from common experiences of members of collectives that are transmitted across generations." Further explanations of culture that follow will be based on these definitions of the concept of culture, which show considerable overlap.

In the management literature, the frameworks and theories of Edward and Mildred Hall, Alexander Thomas, Geert Hofstede, Alfons Trompenaars, Shalom Schwartz and the GLOBE team around Robert House have received particular attention. Müller and Gelbrich (2015) assign the frameworks of the Halls and Alexander Thomas to the qualitative and the other approaches mentioned here to the quantitative. These six approaches to describing and explaining similarities and differences in the cultural orientations of people from different regions or nations were developed in Western cultures.

Hall's Concept of Culture

During their stays in various regions of the world, Hall and Hall observed and documented differences in the social behavior of the cultural groups they visited. Their goal was to identify, define and describe higher-level characteristics along which systematic comparisons of national cultures could be made. A special feature of their approach is the finding that human behavior is largely context-specific. According to Hall (1976; Hall & Hall, 1990), this specification applies in particular to interpersonal communication. Hall (1983) used an auditory metaphor, claiming that, because of their cultural orientations, individuals are tuned to a certain frequency. Therefore, they cannot receive what is being sent on other frequencies.

Moreover, Hall's cultural theorizing (1976, 1981) contains observations on the handling of time and space as well as on the speed of information transmission and processing within societies. The characteristics described by Hall and their respective attributes are summarized in Table 2.1 (adapted from Hall, 1976, 1981, and Hall & Hall, 1990; cf. Müller & Gelbrich, 2015, p. 81).

Table 2.1: Culture dimensions suggested by Hall (1976, 1981; Hall & Hall, 1990).

Communication Situation = Context	Time = Chronemics	Space = Proxemics	Speed of Information Transmission and Processing
low context vs. high context societies	monochrone and future-oriented vs. polychrone and past-oriented societies	low touch vs. high touch societies	slow message societies vs. fast message societies

- Low context versus high context societies: Do the individuals of a culture try to verbally express the object of their communication as precisely as possible (i.e., low context)? Or does the sender limit themself to a few verbal hints, the meaning of which is revealed to the recipient from nonverbal cues and the communication context (i.e., high context)?
- Monochrone versus polychrone societies: How do individuals from different cultures use time as a resource in everyday life? Is time seen as a scarce resource that is used as planned and targeted as possible? Or is the available time viewed as a resource that can be used spontaneously to complete pending tasks and maintain social interactions—often at the same time?

- Low touch versus high touch societies: What degree of physical proximity or distance do members of different cultures prefer in social interaction situations?
- Speed of information transmission and processing: At what speed does information spread in a society or in groups?

In Hall's publications (1976, 1981, 1983) there are no overviews of the cultural dimensions he used to describe regional or national cultures, but a few pieces of information can be found in his books, such as, "American culture, while not on the bottom, is toward the lower end of the scale. We are still considerably above the German-Swiss, the Germans, and the Scandinavians in the amount of 'contexting' needed in everyday life. . . . China, the possessor of a great and complex culture, is on the high-context end of the scale" (Hall, 1976, p. 91). From this and from additional descriptions by Morden (1999), Usunier (2000) and Kotabe and Helsen (2001), van Everdingen and Waarts (2003, p. 23) have developed a ranking scale of cultural orientation along Hall's context dimension, which is shown in Table 2.2.

Table 2.2: Ranking scale of cultural orientation along Hall's context dimension (adapted from van Everdingen & Waarts, 2003).

Type of Society	Rank	Countries/Regions	Characteristics
Low context Societies	1	Germany, Switzerland, Austria	– exchange of explicitly formulated messages
	2	New Zealand, South Africa (Whites)	– comprehension of messages is based on what is said or written
	3	USA (White Anglosaxon Protestants), Canada	– information seeking in publicly accessible sources (reports, Internet, data bases, etc.)
	4	Norway, Sweden, Denmark, Finland	
	5	UK, Australia	
	6	Benelux Countries	
	7	USA (Blacks, Hispanics, Asians)	
	8	Slavic Countries	
High context Societies	9	Other Middle European Countries	– comprehension of messages is based on context cues
	10	South Korea, South-East Asia	
	11	India and Indian subcontinent	– information status is perceived as perfect after information seeking in private network
	12	Arabic Countries, Africa	
	13	Latin America	
	14	France, Portugal, European Countries along the Mediterranean Sea Coast	
	15	China	
	16	Japan	

This overview reveals clear differences between German and other Central and Northern European societies on the one hand and Chinese society on the other along the cultural characteristic of context suggested by Hall—Germany is one of the low context societies; China is definitely one of the high context societies. Significant differences between Germans and Chinese in information-seeking behavior and in sending and receiving messages should be expected.

Hall's ideas have been and are still being discussed in the literature on international management more than 70 years after their publication, perhaps not least because of their high level of vividness. In his descriptive publications, Hall uses numerous anecdotes to illustrate the cultural dimensions he introduced. Nevertheless, his presentations remain highly opaque from a methodological point of view. There is no documentation of his approach to identifying the four cultural dimensions in his writings, nor are his explanations suitable for clearly operationalizing these dimensions. Empirical evidence for the cultural descriptions of individual nations proposed by Hall is lacking, as are attempts by other authors to empirically validate these descriptions. Work published by William Gudykunst is one of the few exceptions (Gudykunst, Ting-Toomey & Chua, 1988).

Thomas's Concept of Culture

Thomas introduces culture as a meaningful orientation system for the members of a nation or society (Thomas, 2003). In the qualitative cultural approach he formulated, he differentiated between central and peripheral cultural standards. He describes these standards as "all ways of perceiving, thinking, evaluating and acting which the majority of the members of a nation regard as normal, typical and obligatory for themselves and for others" (Thomas, 2003, p. 25). They serve to assess the behavior observed in others as well as to assess one's own behavior. Central standards are used largely independent of the situation, while peripheral standards relate to specific areas of behavior or situations defined in terms of place, time, people involved and, if necessary, other features of context. When an individual or group violates core cultural standards, negative interpersonal and social responses (detachment, rejection, sanctions, etc.) are likely to result.

The assessment of behavior as "normal" or "deviant" must always be understood in relation to a reference group. This group's composition influences which cultural standards are used, which observed behaviors are perceived as culture-conforming or deviant and, if applicable, which negative or positive reactions are shown in response. The relativity of cultural standards becomes clear, for example, when the behavior of German managers is described from the point of view of foreign observers. A member of Thomas's team has compiled statements from respondents of French, Czech, US American and Chinese origin (see Table 2.3; adapted from Schroll-Machl, 2003, p. 73 based on Demangeat & Molz, 2003, Schroll-Machl, 2001, Markowsky &

Thomas, 1995, Thomas & Schenk, 2001 and Thomas, Schenk & Heisel, 2008; cf. also Müller & Gelbrich, 2015, p. 87).

Table 2.3: German cultural standards as perceived by French, Czech, US-American and Chinese observers.

German Cultural Standards as Perceived by . . .			
French	**Czech**	**US-Americans**	**Chinese**
explicit, direct communication	low context communication, confrontative conflict style	direct interpersonal communication	direct, truthful communication
rule-oriented, stability-oriented	structure-oriented	rule-oriented, need for organizing processes	rule-oriented, contracts are binding
separation of private and work spheres	separation of private and work spheres	private sphere is separated, interpersonal distance differs across social categories	separation of private and work spheres
systematic settlement of tasks	prefer consecutiveness		monochrone time orientation
object-oriented	object-oriented	private property matters	object-oriented
self-regulated	rule-based control of life	conscientiousness	
civil equality is aspired to			
	self-confidence		
			trusting in authorities
			gender roles are differentiated
sense of solidarity			individualism

Three examples from Table 2.3 show the relativity of cultural standards with particular clarity:

- Chinese observers note unvarnished and open communication among Germans. In China, saving face is an important goal in interpersonal communication. Maintaining social order and harmonious relationships often requires hiding an unpleasant truth. Against this background, the preference of Germans to describe things truthfully is obviously particularly striking.
- Collectivistically oriented Chinese observers are particularly struck by the individualistic orientation of the Germans. On the other hand, observers from the

Czech Republic, France and the USA do not mention this feature because it largely corresponds to their cultural standards.

- Chinese observers mention the monochronic time planning as a conspicuous cultural feature of the Germans. French and Czech observers also mentioned this feature in a slightly different way, but not so US observers, for whom monochronic time planning should be self-evident.

The cultural standards approach introduced by Thomas (2003) suggests that while there may be typical and stable characteristics of members of a nation (or ethnic group within a nation) in terms of character, the description of such character varies depending on an observer's own cultural orientation. Characteristics that are markedly different from the observer's own cultural standards are likely to be used when foreign national characters are characterized. With regard to the differences between German and Chinese managers to be examined in this work, Table 2.3 already gives some clear indications.

With his approach, Thomas (2003) influenced the relevant discussions only slightly. Elaborations and applications of his concept have not yet been made. In the English-speaking world, his contribution has hardly been noticed. A critical point to note about this approach, however, is that the basic findings of Thomas's research team carry the potential for unjustifiably confirming cultural stereotypes.

Hofstede's Concept of Culture

The foundation of quantitative approaches to explaining cultural differences is essentially achieved by empirically recording the values typical of the inhabitants of a country and summarizing them into a few dimensions using factor analysis. Individual countries can then be positioned in the multidimensional cultural spaces created in this way, and ideal-typical national cultures can be described and compared.[1]

Among the quantitative approaches to explaining cultural differences, the framework suggested by Hofstede is probably one of the most influential models. The basis for Hofstede's first data evaluations were the results of an employee survey at IBM,

---

1 In general, equating country or nation and culture within this approach seems problematic. In many countries, uniform "national cultures" could develop, be it because of the size of the country in terms of area or population (Russia, China), because of multilingualism (Switzerland) or the different historical development of parts of the country (East and West Germany, North and South Korea). In addition, structures of cultural dimensions that are observable at the aggregated (country) level cannot always be replicated at the individual survey level (e.g., Yoo, Donthu, & Lenartowicz, 2011). Nevertheless, the findings of quantitative cultural approaches help to better understand differences between country cultures.

which was carried out in 72 IBM branches in 40 countries from 1966 to 1973 (Hermes IBM Attitude Survey). The aim was to survey work-related values, perceptions of working life and personal goals of IBM employees as well as their job satisfaction (Hofstede, 1980). In a further survey wave, the study was extended to 50 countries, data from approximately 116,000 IBM employees were analyzed using multivariate statistical, in particular, factor-analytical, methods. In initial publications (Hofstede, 1980, 1983), Hofstede presented four cultural dimensions: (1) acceptance of power distance, (2) individualism vs. collectivism, (3) masculinity vs. femininity and (4) uncertainty avoidance. A few years later, after further data collection, which could now also be carried out including Chinese respondents, the four-dimensional framework was supplemented by a fifth dimension, which was initially called "Confucian dynamics" and later "long-term vs. short-term orientation" (Hofstede & Bond, 1988). The Hofstede approach was further supplemented by the introduction of a sixth cultural dimension "indulgence vs. restraint." This was based on data from the World Values Survey collected in 93 countries (Minkov, 2007, 2011; Hofstede, Hofstede & Minkov, 2010).

To describe the relative differences between country cultures, Hofstede (1992) reports index values for all cultural dimensions, the absolute values of which are irrelevant (Müller & Gelbrich, 2015). Table 2.4 shows index values for Germany (D) and China (PRC).

Table 2.4: Index values of Hofstede's cultural dimensions for Germany and PRC.[2]

Nation	Cultural Dimensions					
	Power Distance	Individualism/ Collectivism	Masculinity / Femininity	Uncertainty Avoidance	Long Term vs. Short Term Orientation	Indulgence vs. Restraint
D	35	67	66	65	83	40
PRC	80	20	66	30	87	24

A comparison of the index values for both nations shows a very high degree of similarity with regard to the cultural dimensions "masculinity vs. femininity"[3] and "long-term vs. short-term orientation"[4] as well as moderate degree of similarity with regard

---

2 Source: www.hofstede-insights.com/country-comparison/china,germany/, accessed June 13, 2023.
3 The index value of 66 indicates success-oriented societies in which status is shown by appropriate symbols.
4 The index values of 83 and 87 indicate a dominant pragmatic orientation of the societies. Perseverance, ambition and thrift characterize the individual behavior in many situations.

to the cultural dimension "indulgence vs. restraint."[5] Significant differences in the index values are shown for the remaining three cultural dimensions:[6]

– Power Distance: A relatively high index value of 80 is reported for China. A clear majority of the population takes the position that inequalities between people are acceptable. The relationship between superiors and subordinates is clearly structured hierarchically and there is no protection against abuse of power by superiors. Individuals are sanctioned by formal authority and are generally optimistic about people's ability to lead and initiate. It is generally believed that people should limit themselves to aspirations appropriate to their rank.

   Germany has a rather low index value of 35 for this cultural dimension. German society is organized on a federal basis and is supported by a strong middle class. Co-determination rights are comparatively extensive and must be taken into account by employers. A direct and participatory style of communication is common. Control measures in companies are often dispensed with. Individuals with managerial functions are most likely to be accepted, if they have specialist knowledge and can apply this knowledge successfully.

– Individualism/Collectivism: The index value of 20 for China signals a clear collectivist orientation in the Chinese society. Individuals tend to put their self-interest second to the interests of their ingroup(s). Group affiliations influence attitudes towards many everyday objects and topics. In smaller companies, members of the in-group (e.g., family members) are given preferential treatment when it comes to promotions. Employee loyalty to their organization tends to be low, but does not necessarily appear so to the people in the organization. While relations with ingroup members are cooperative, they are cold or even hostile towards outgroup members. Personal relationships in the network of ingroups take precedence over performing civic functions for society.

   German society is clearly individualistic (index value 67). The most common social structure is small families with a focus on the parent–child relationship and not on other relatives, such as aunts and uncles. Self-actualization is considered an ideal. Loyalty is based on personal preferences for people and a sense of duty and responsibility. The framework for this characteristic is the employment contract concluded between the employer and the employee. Interpersonal communication is characterized by a high degree of directness and explicitness. It fol-

---

5 Index scores of 24 and 40, respectively, indicate that in both societies, self-control dominates everyday behavior, which is guided by multifarious social norms, and in which sacrifices of extensive rewards for achievement is practiced.

6 The following depictions on the nations of Germany and the People's Republic of China summarize explanations given on the Hofstede Insights website, www.hofstede-insights.com, accessed March 20, 2023.

lows the motto, "Honest, even if it hurts!" If mistakes happen, the person who caused them usually gets a fair chance to learn from these mistakes.

– Uncertainty Avoidance: For China, a rather low index value of 30 is reported for this cultural dimension. This means that in China people are relaxed about uncertainties. Of course, social life is determined by rules and laws, but compliance with them is often handled in a flexible and situation-oriented manner (cf., e.g., Clissold, 2014). These include a high degree of pragmatism and a high tolerance for ambiguity. These behavioral tendencies are sometimes interpreted as reflecting Daoist heritage. The Chinese language is full of ambiguities that are often difficult for people from other cultures to understand. The Chinese are often seen as adaptable and entrepreneurial.

Germany is one of the societies whose members try to avoid uncertainties (index value 65). Borrowing from the philosophical legacy of Kant, Hegel and Fichte, deductive approaches are strongly favored over inductive approaches, whether in thinking, planning or presenting an argument. A systematic overview is often a prerequisite for action. This precision is also reflected in the legal system. Clarification of details is important because it gives assurance that a particular topic or project has been well thought out. Germans compensate for their greater insecurity by hoping that applying expertise will lead to good results.

Based on the index values for the four cultural dimensions initially formulated by Hofstede (1980), Kogut and Singh (1988) proposed a measure of the cultural distance between two nations or societies (Thomas & Peterson, 2018; Cuypers et al., 2018; Konara & Mohr, 2019). Taking these four cultural dimensions into account, a Kogut–Singh index value of 2.9 is reported for the cultural distance between Germany and China (Müller & Gelbrich, 2015). The cultural distance index according to Kogut and Singh can attain values between 0 and 6.[7]

The German cultural scientist Hansen is quoted here as representative of the many, often harsh words of criticism of Hofstede's work: "All in all, his book is a catastrophe for modern cultural studies. He sins against all the progress that has been made since the 1960s and it was precisely this hodgepodge that taught the unteachable, who considered the concept of culture to be nonsense. Those psychologists, sociologists and economists who only trust empirical analyses were convinced by Hofstede's statistics that culture consists of hard facts that can be measured and weighed" (Hansen, 2000, p. 285). In addition to such words of fundamental criticism, discussions about the informative value of Hofstede's studies also start with the questionnaire items he used and

---

7 Konara and Mohr (2019) have recently shown that the index in its original form overestimates small cultural distances, while underestimating large cultural distances. A conclusive assessment of the validity of various indices for measuring cultural distances between nations cannot and should not be made within the scope of this work. Since the index value of cultural distance between Germany and China is in the medium value range, it can be assumed that the Kogut–Singh Index reflects this distance sufficiently well.

the interpretation of the answers of his subjects. Further points of criticism relate to the representativeness of the subjects and the apparent lack of a theoretical basis for the derivation of the cultural dimensions. However, numerous replications of Hofstede's work show the robustness of his findings (e.g., Söndergaard, 1994; however, Minkov & Kaasa, 2022, recently proposed a two-dimensional structure based on World Values Survey data with individualism/collectivism and long-term orientation as cultural dimensions), which have significantly structured and influenced the research map of intercultural management theory over the past decades.

Trompenaars's Concept of Culture

The Dutch management consultant Trompenaars, together with the British economist Hampden-Turner, proposed a cultural approach with seven cultural dimensions (Hampden-Turner & Trompenaars, 1993; Trompenaars & Hampden-Turner, 1997), which was formulated with respect to structures and processes in companies. The empirical basis for this approach was survey results. Trompenaars collected his survey data among participants of his management seminars. He claims that responses from more than 15,000 managers from all parts of the world were taken into account. In the surveys, respondents are confronted with descriptions of numerous situations. They are then asked to state their probable reaction to each situation based on given alternative courses of action. Precise information on the individual situations used, the given alternative answers and the results can only be found sparsely in Trompenaars' publications (e.g., Hampden-Turner & Trompenaars, 1993), which is why doubts about the validity and reliability of the data used by Trompenaars were often expressed (e.g., Hofstede, 1996). From the answers given by their respondents, Trompenaars and Hampden-Turner derived seven value-based cultural dimensions (Hampden-Turner & Trompenaars, 1993; Trompenaars, 1993):

- Individualism vs. Communitarianism: Similar to Hofstede (1980), Trompenaars describes individualism as a basic orientation towards the ego and communitarianism as a basic orientation towards the goals and specifications of the community. "[A] vital requirement of all work organizations is the provision of care, attention, information, and support to each of its individual members, while assuring that the needs of the community and the organization are well served by these individuals. [. . .] The 'integrity' of the organization depends in part on how well the individualism of employees, shareholders, and customers is reconciled with the communitarianism of the larger system" (Hampden-Turner & Trompenaars, 1993, p. 8).
- Universalism vs. Particularism: In universalistic cultures, the obligation to meet the standards in which one's own culture agrees without looking at the individual case is in the foreground. Particular cultures emphasize the particular obligations that an individual may have to an individual or group in the particular circum-

stances of a given situation (Trompenaars, 1993). "Business organizations in all fields of enterprise need to create rules, codes, procedures, and routines. . . . But this alone is inadequate. Organizations must also discover swiftly any case that is exceptional, that reveals a rule's limitations and hence merits particular attention. Unless they do this their rules and procedures will progressively lose touch . . . with changing environments. . . . The 'integrity' of the enterprise . . . must depend in part on how well universalism (rules of wide generality) is reconciled with particularism (special exceptions)" (Hampden-Turner & Trompenaars, 1993, p. 7).

– Time orientation: Economic organizations have to coordinate numerous processes in order to be able to react successfully to the requirements of other market participants. On the one hand, this cultural dimension should reflect the willingness and ability to run many of these processes simultaneously (synchronously) and to make them marketable offers. On the other hand, the time orientation of decision-makers in companies also describes their tendency to consider the past, present and future in their decisions and actions (Hampden-Turner & Trompenaars, 1993).

– Neutrality vs. Emotionality: In more neutral cultures, individuals make great efforts to control their emotions. Their actions are far more reason-based than emotion-based. Individuals in more neutral cultures do not reveal what they think or feel. It is important to them to maintain the appearance of self-control. In contrast, in more emotional cultures it is considered natural to show spontaneous emotions in the course of one's professional activities. Such expressions of feelings may even be desired.

– Ascribed vs. achieved status: Individuals can acquire or "earn" status and respect by virtue of their individual contributions to organizational performance. However, they can also be accorded status and respect without referring to their individual achievements; in this case, status and respect are acquired by attribution according to the prevalent rules in an organization.[8]

– Separation between spheres of life: Social relationships are either entered into and maintained in a specific sphere of life or cultivated across spheres of life. Trompenaars (1993) characterizes cultures in which these relationships differ in the individual spheres of life as specific cultures. In diffuse cultures, on the other hand, many social relationships from work life also exist in the private life of individuals.

---

8 "All business organizations require for their effective operation that status, position, and respect be given to those persons who have succeeded on behalf of the enterprise. It is obviously in the interests of any corporation that those who have performed best rise to positions of greater influence, there to surpass their former achievements and set an example to others. Rewards should be commensurate with contributions. But definitions of what is worth achieving in the first place must be set by the organization" (Hampden-Turner & Trompenaars, 1993, p. 9).

– Environmental orientation: This cultural dimension focuses on the "locus of control" perceived by individuals. When individuals perceive more internal control, they are guided by the impression that they can influence and even control their environment (and also the forces of nature) in order to achieve their goals. On the other hand, if the impression that nature or their environment controls them dominates, then the insight arises that they have to work in harmony with their environment in order to achieve goals (Thomas & Peterson, 2018). At work or in relationships, individuals align their actions with others and avoid conflict where possible.

In summary, it can be stated that Trompenaars' approach shows striking similarities to Hofstede's approach. This is not surprising given that Trompenaars was a student of Hofstede. Since Trompenaars never comprehensively documented his data base and his methodological approach, his approach is still viewed with skepticism in the relevant sciences. Nevertheless, it has found its way into practical seminars on intercultural management in a variety of ways because of its rich, practical features. Therefore, it seems reasonable to take a closer look at the similarities and differences between the two approaches.

The cultural dimensions of Hofstede's and Trompenaars' culture concepts overlap but also differ. Trompenaars's approach lacks cultural dimensions that could express the power distance and uncertainty avoidance of Hofstede's approach. Conversely, there are no counterparts in Hofstede's approach for three of the dimensions of Trompenaars' approach. Table 2.5 shows the overlaps and differences between the two concepts (based on Soares, Farhangmehr & Shoham, 2007).

Table 2.5: Overlaps and differences between the culture concepts suggested by Hofstede and Trompenaars.

Hofstede	Trompenaars
Masculinity/Femininity	Neutrality vs. Emotionality
Individualism/Collectivism	1) Individualism/Communitarianism 2) Universalism/Particularism
Power Distance	
Uncertainty Avoidance	
Long-Term vs. Short-Term Orientation	Time Orientation
Indulgence vs. Restraint	
	1) Separation between Spheres of Life 2) Ascribed vs. Achieved Status 3) Environmental Orientation

Trompenaars' publications do not contain any comprehensive country comparisons along the seven cultural dimensions. However, his approach is applied by many users to structure their individual assessments of cultural differences between individual countries. Such labels for individual countries often differ significantly from one another. This inconsistency also applies to Germany and the People's Republic of China. Table 2.6 summarizes the characteristics of the national cultures of both countries (cf. also Hampden-Turner & Trompenaars, 1996).

Table 2.6: Description of German and Chinese national cultures along seven cultural dimensions suggested by Trompenaars.

Cultural Dimensions Suggested by Trompenaars	Germany	China
Individualism vs. Communitarianism	rather individualistic orientation	communitarian orientation
Universalism vs. Particularism	universalism	particularism
Time Orientation	future-oriented, sequential sense of time	future-oriented, synchronous sense of time
Neutrality vs. Emotionality	rather emotional	rather neutral
Ascribed vs. Achieved Status	status achieved by individual performance	status ascribed according to established rules of society
Separation between Spheres of Life	diffuse	rather specific
Environmental Orientation	unclear	external locus of control or secondary control is predominant

While the culture model proposed by Trompenaars has found its way into the economics literature (e.g., DeBurca, Fletcher, & Brown, 2004; Mead & Andrews, 2009; Perlitz & Schrank, 2013; Thomas & Peterson, 2018), the impact of this approach on research as well as on teaching is rather limited—not least due to the incomplete empirical database. Trompenaars uses the model in the course of his extensive consulting work and in the management seminars he offers and seems to have little interest in scientific discourse. With his model, Trompenaars draws attention to individual areas of life (e.g., universalism vs. particularism, attribution of status vs. acquisition of status, separation between spheres of life) that have received little or no consideration in other cultural models (Smith, Trompenaars & Dugan, 1995; Smith & Dugan, 1996).

Schwartz's Concept of Culture

Schwartz developed a "theory of universal cultural values" in the 1990s. To this end, he defines values as "conceptions of the desirable that guide the way social actors (e.g., organizational leaders, policymakers, individual persons, etc.) select actions, evaluate people and events, and explain their actions and evaluations" (Schwartz, 1999, p. 24). In this context, he also speaks of values as "guiding principles" for the life of individuals and groups (Schwartz, 1994b). The starting point of Schwartz's reasoning is the consideration that human societies worldwide are challenged to overcome three fundamental problems characteristic of all societies. These include maintaining a functioning social order, dealing with the natural and social environment and striving for a balanced relationship between the individual and the group (Schwartz, 1992). Based on empirical surveys of teachers and students from 38 countries, Schwartz extracted a two-dimensional metastructure of values (Schwartz & Bilsky, 1990; Schwartz & Huismans, 1995) along the dimensions of openness vs. conservatism and self-enhancement vs. self-transcendence. The following values are assigned to the poles of these two dimensions as a result of multidimensional scaling (see Figure 2.3). A value circle comprising ten value types is based on that:

– Openness to Change: Hedonism, Stimulation, Self-Direction
– Conservation: Security, Conformity, Tradition
– Self-Enhancement: Achievement, Power
– Self-Transcendence: Universalism, Benevolence

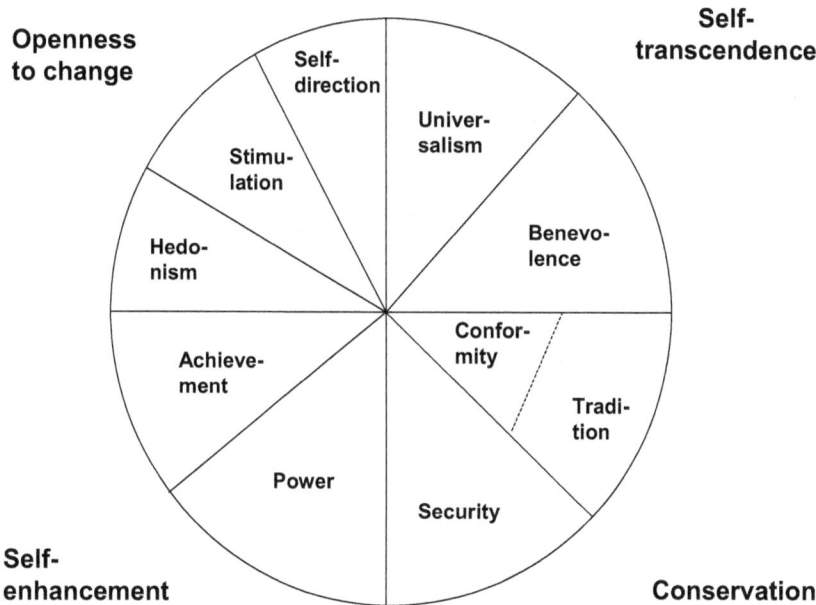

Figure 2.3: Ten value types suggested by Schwartz (1994b, p. 24) based on Schwartz (1992).

In later publications, Schwartz presented a revised cultural model with seven value domains (Conservatism, Harmony, Egalitarianism, Intellectual Autonomy, Affective Autonomy, Mastery, and Hierarchy) that was validated based on data from about 50 countries (Schwartz, 1994a, 1999). These value types were arranged along the three dimensions of conservatism vs. intellectual and emotional autonomy, hierarchy vs. egalitarianism, and harmony vs. mastery (see Figure 2.4; Schwartz, 1999).

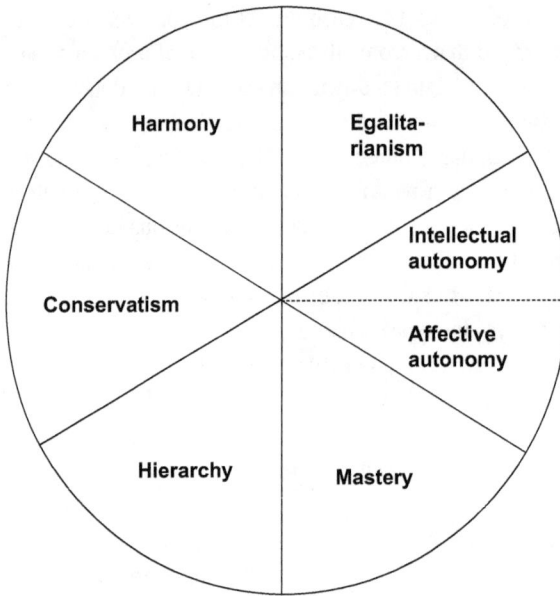

Figure 2.4: Seven value domains suggested by Schwartz (1999, p. 30).

Based on these types of values, Schwartz (1999) defines four cultural areas: Western Europe, Eastern Europe, English-speaking countries, and the Far East. According to his judgment, Schwartz sees a high relevance in the Western European countries of intellectual autonomy and equality; in Far Eastern countries, of hierarchy. According to him, assessing similarities and differences between the dominant types of values in individual countries or regions could help to better understand tensions between nations and to show ways of successful international understanding (Schwartz, 2008).

Overall, Schwartz's value model can be seen as an advance over the Hofstede approach, since value interdependencies are taken into account in this later model. Schwartz examines the charged and complementary relationships between values and explains how they develop, postulating a dynamic value structure. Schwartz's model is only slowly finding its way into international management theory and research (see, e.g., Müller & Gelbrich, 2015; Thomas & Peterson, 2018).

The Culture Concept of the GLOBE Study

Similar to Hofstede, A. Thomas, and Trompenaars, the authors of the so-called GLOBE study also deal with the causes and characteristics of cultural differences. GLOBE stands for the Global Leadership and Organizational Behavior Effectiveness Research Program. The study focuses on the question: "To what extent are leadership styles influenced by national cultures?" The GLOBE study represents the most up-to-date, comprehensive and meaningful research approach in intercultural management.

The GLOBE study was initiated in 1993 and carried out by an international research group under the leadership of the organizational psychologist, Robert J. House. The sample included 17,300 middle-level management team members from 951 com-

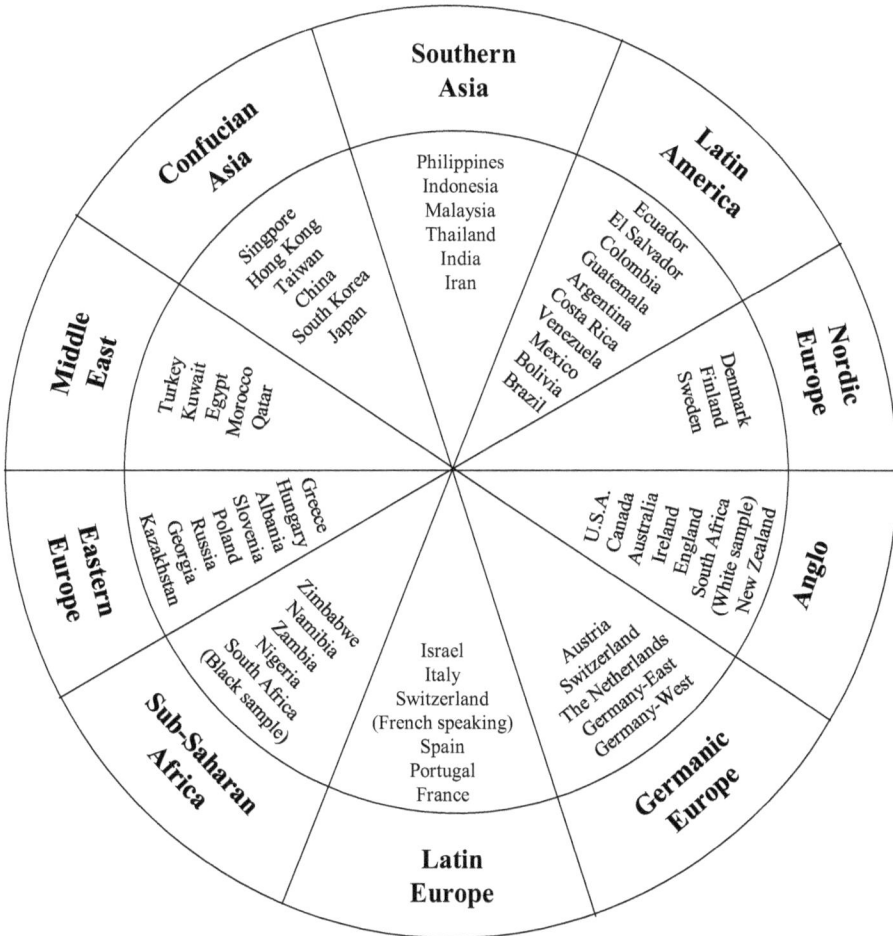

Figure 2.5: Country cluster of the GLOBE study (House et al., 2004, p. 190).

panies located in 62 countries or regions worldwide (House et al., 2004). The GLOBE study is based on Hofstede's approach and develops it further.

The country cultures examined were grouped into ten country clusters or culture groups (see Figure 2.5). Based on the GLOBE data, nine value dimensions were identified with which the cultural profile of a culture can be described, namely performance orientation, future orientation, gender equality, assertiveness, institutional collectivism, group-related collectivism, power distance, humane orientation, and uncertainty avoidance. The value dimensions are examined on two levels: "Practices (As Is)" is about determining the respective attitudes and behavior of the respondents in terms of a description of the respondents' working situation as it is. "Values (As Should Be)" provide information about how these attitudes and behaviors should ideally be from the point of view of the respondents, that is, in terms of what should be.

Individual cultures were also examined for the prevailing leadership styles. Table 2.7 provides an overview of the leadership styles.

Table 2.7: Leadership styles across cultures identified in the GLOBE-Study (House et al., 2004, p. 14).

1. **Charismatic/Value-Based Leadership**
charismatic and value based → inspiring, motivating, achievement-oriented
2. **Team-Oriented Leadership**
team oriented → diplomatic, integrating
3. **Participative Leadership**
participative → involving others in decisions
4. **Human-Oriented Leadership**
humane → humble, passionate
5. **Autonomous Leadership**
autonomous → independent, individualistic
6. **Self-Protective Leadership**
Self-protective → status-conscious, self-centered

Nine value-based cultural dimensions are distinguished in the GLOBE study (House & Javidan, 2004; Perlitz & Schrank, 2013; Müller & Gelbrich, 2015; Thomas & Peterson, 2018) as follows:

– Performance Orientation:
   Achievement and achievement motivation are among the decisive, determining factors of modern industrial societies (McClelland, 1966). So, the cultural conditions and consequences of performance orientation are particularly examined by GLOBE.

   The results produced by the GLOBE team of authors confirm in many ways the influence of achievement motivation on the economic and social development of countries and cultures. According to GLOBE, in performance-oriented societies, performance outcomes are valued more highly than social relationships; assertiveness and competitiveness are given higher priority than social harmony. Furthermore, performance orientation coincides with a preference for direct communication—to name just a few key distinguishing features.

According to the GLOBE study, the charismatic, but also the participatory leadership model is frequently used in performance-oriented cultures.

– Future Orientation:
Similar to Hofstede, the GLOBE team identified future orientation as a cultural dimension that focuses specifically on the time orientation of individuals, organizations and cultures. Cultures that are characterized by a strong focus on the future differ significantly from cultures with a weak focus on the future. This emphasis is shown, e.g., in differing attitudes to success, a different propensity to save and the different relevance of strategic thinking.

Humane leadership is the predominant leadership style in future-oriented cultures.

– Gender Egalitarianism:
Similar to Hofstede, the GLOBE study also shows that different perceptions of gender roles are a key feature illustrating cultural differences. In so-called feminine cultures, flat organizations, a high appreciation of quality of life, and solidarity can be observed. The so-called masculine cultures are more hierarchically organized and results oriented.

Both the charismatic leadership style and the participatory leadership style are common in feminine cultures.

– Assertiveness:
Assertiveness is a cultural dimension that was identified exclusively in the GLOBE study. House and his team of authors found that there are cultures in which assertiveness or dominant and assertive behavior is particularly valued. Strong self-confidence often coincides with admiration of strong personalities and appreciating success and progress. In many other cultures, however, less importance is attached to assertiveness.

Both the humane and the authoritarian leadership style are particularly widespread in assertive cultures.

– Institutional Collectivism and In-Group Collectivism:
Similar to other conceptualizations of culture, the GLOBE study has shown various connections between the cultural dimension of collectivism and the attitudes and behavior that are shaped by it at the level of societies and organizations. In addition, an extended approach was developed by the GLOBE study, which distinguishes two forms of collectivism. These are called Collectivism I (Institutional Collectivism) and Collectivism II (In-Group Collectivism).

Institutional collectivism expresses whether and to what extent collectivist goals are realized in a society at the macro level, e.g., through state or union-determined redistribution policies. Accordingly, an indicator of institutional collectivism is a strongly developed state social policy in a country. This means that the state, through its institutions, is primarily geared towards distribution-oriented goals (as, for example, in the Scandinavian countries).

Group-internal collectivism, on the other hand, means what we commonly understand by collectivism, namely a strong orientation towards the specifications and goals of the group or community.

Consequently, it is possible for a culture to be collectivistic on the macro-social level (e.g., through a state redistribution policy in the welfare state) and individualistic on the micro-social level (example Sweden). In contrast, countries influenced by Confucian philosophy tend to be positioned high on both collectivism scales.

The results of the GLOBE study show that the leadership model preferred in in-group collectivist cultures is the team-oriented leadership style.

– Power Distance:
Similar to Hofstede, the GLOBE team considers the power imbalance that prevails in any society to be a cultural dimension that is expressed differently in different cultural systems; attitudes and dealings with power and status vary greatly from culture to culture. Social stratification in high power distance countries is clearly hierarchical and social mobility is often restricted. High power distance often coincides with corruption and a curtailment of civil rights. In contrast, cultures with a low power distance have a large middle class, their social mobility is high, concern about civil rights is prominent and corruption is relatively low.

The data of the GLOBE study indicate that an authoritarian leadership style is preferred in high power-distance cultures. In some cultures, it appears as a paternalistic leadership model that also contains authoritarian elements, including leadership by "carrot and stick."

– Humane Orientation:
Human orientation is also a central value dimension of human thought and action. Many religions and worldviews contain norms and values that are geared towards human goodness, as in the Confucian code of ethics, e.g., *ren* (仁), i.e., human heartedness. The GLOBE study uncovered a number of relationships in this regard. So, in the organizations of cultures that are particularly humane in their orientation, informal relationships, cooperation in groups and social responsibility are particularly valued.

With regard to a preferred leadership style, the GLOBE study found that a humane orientation is often combined with a leadership style that is characterized by team spirit and interpersonal orientation.

– Uncertainty Avoidance:
Quite frequently individuals are confronted with life situations whose outcome is open and uncertain. Religion, philosophy and technology have produced a variety of

concepts that aim to make life for individuals and society calculable, predictable and thus less unsafe. At the organizational level, bureaucracy represents such a stabilizing social environment. The GLOBE study shows that uncertainty-avoiding societies are more likely to formalize the behavior of its members, value order and resist change.

With regard to the preferred leadership style, the results of the GLOBE study indicate a close correlation between uncertainty avoidance and team-oriented or humane leadership.

The GLOBE Lens Applied to German and Chinese Cultures

Figure 2.6 shows how the German national culture is perceived by managers working there. We see clear differences between the actual ("As Is") and the desired ("As Should Be") values. It shows that the German respondents want a value constellation that is characterized by a less pronounced avoidance of uncertainty, less assertiveness and at the same time a clear increase in employee orientation, equality, and solidarity in business and society.

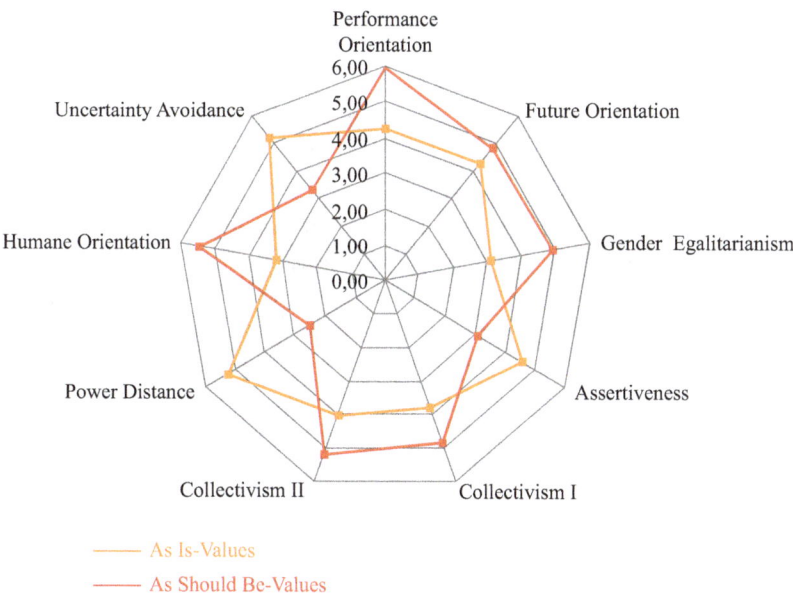

Figure 2.6: Comparison of As Is-Values and As Should Be-Values for Germany (adapted from House et al., 2004).

The comparison of the As Is-Values for China and Germany is also insightful (see Figure 2.7). Particularly large differences can be seen in the assessments of collectivism (in both variants) and human orientation. Confucian influences could ex-

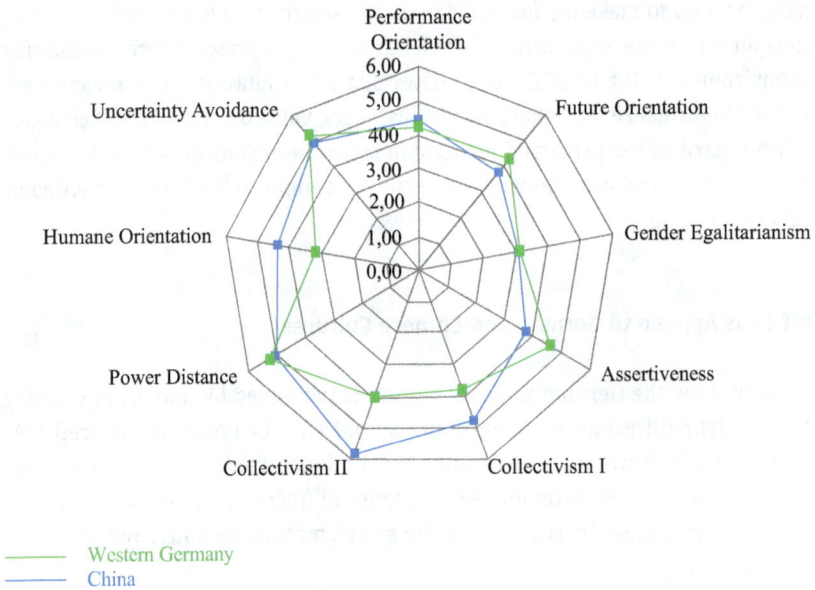

Figure 2.7: Comparison of As Is-Values for Western Germany and China (adapted from House et al., 2004; source of data: GLOBE, 2021a and 2021b).

plain the corresponding values for China. They will be considered in greater detail in Chapter 3.

Using the central thesis of convergence theory, the research team of the GLOBE study investigated the question of whether and to what extent cultures are merging into a uniform world culture in the context of globalization. With a view to leadership-theoretical considerations, the question then arises as to whether ideas are developing in the direction of a universally preferred leadership style in the various cultures. Both questions addressed by House et al. (2004) are answered with a clear "no."

The quote from Blaise Pascal (1623–1662) that Hofstede used to preface his epochal work, *Culture's consequences*, published in 1980, is therefore still valid: "Vérité en-deça des Pyrénées, erreur au-delà." ("There are truths on this side of the Pyrenees which are falsehoods on the other."). The same truth applies in the case of preferred management styles. Here, too, the results of the GLOBE study can be interpreted as showing that each cultural group has its own ideas about optimal leadership style: According to the study, managers in each individual country have more or less implicit ideas about which pattern of leadership qualities is particularly efficient and therefore optimal for its respective cultural group. Despite these differences, it is striking that the charismatic leadership model is one of the preferred leadership styles in many countries. Answering the question of whether this finding indicates that, despite the worldwide diversity of types of leadership that are considered efficient, something like a universal idea of ideal leadership exists is left to future research.

It is noteworthy that the topic of "trust" is only briefly addressed on four pages of the approximately 2000 pages of the publication of the GLOBE study. Hopefully, greater importance will be attached to the issue of trust in the announced continuation of the research approach initiated by GLOBE.

The operationalizations and culture descriptions found in the GLOBE approach for individual countries have rarely been considered in cross-cultural economics (Okazaki & Mueller, 2007; Venaik & Brewer, 2010). This oversight may be due to the fact that the measured values for the cultural dimensions on the actual and the desired levels do not show the expected positive correlations, and the reasons for this unexpected result are still unclear (Earley, 2006; Hofstede, 2006; Smith, 2006; Maseland & van Hoorn, 2009). Müller and Gelbrich (2015) discuss six possible explanations for this finding and conclude that a convincing explanation has not yet been found. In any case, the 'onion assumption' as a bracket between the two value levels does not seem to be confirmed empirically. On the other hand, the operationalizations of the GLOBE approach suggest that the managers surveyed did not state their own cultural ideas, but rather indicated what is considered desirable in their respective societies.

Intermediate Result

After reviewing the value-based approaches to describe culture suggested by Hall, Thomas, Hofstede, Trompenaars, Schwartz and House et al. there is considerable evidence that there is a rather large cultural distance between Germany and China. The differences observed relate to the categorical and hierarchical structures of the social systems, the forms of verbal and non-verbal communication, the extent of the separation between different areas of life and rules of status attribution and status acquisition.

It is noteworthy that the frameworks presented so far for describing and explaining cultural differences between (usually nationally defined) cultures refer to the conceptualization of culture mainly shaped by social scientists working from Western cultural traditions. The cultural dimensions differentiated in the individual frameworks were derived from cultural analyses carried out by social scientists with a Western cultural background.

Culture from a Chinese Perspective

In addition to the Western perspective, this work also focuses on the Chinese perspective on the concept of culture. The Chinese equivalent for the word "culture" consists of two Chinese characters that come from the Shang Dynasty (16th–12th century BC), making them among the oldest Chinese characters (Hong & Shouxiang, 2009). The first character (文, wen) means "variegated and interlocking veins" in Classical Chinese (Zhu, 2006). Over the course of many centuries, the meaning of this character has changed; it expresses language, artistic beauty, music, literature and morality (Hong & Shouxiang, 2009). The second character (化, hua) means transformation, change, fusion and education in ancient as well as in modern Chinese (Zhu, 2006).

Over a period of about 2,800 years, the classic Chinese concept of culture has stood for measures of cultivation and civilization of people through education and rituals, literature and music. Culture was seen as opposing violence and barbarism and was given both political and moral meaning (Hong & Shouxiang, 2009). In the 19th century the "ti yong concept" (体用) was developed. According to that, a Chinese society with Chinese culture as the essence (体, ti) and Western cultural elements for practical application (用, yong) should be aimed at (Li, 1994). During this time, numerous works with culture-defining content that were created in Western cultures were translated into Chinese. At about the same time, treatises on culture emerged in China from different perspectives, each with their own definitions of culture. According to Hong and Shouxiang (2009), these approaches can each be assigned to one of the following categories:

- Culture in a broader sense: In the approaches assigned to this category of meaning, culture is distinguished from nature. Culture is what humankind has created and what enables humane life. The level of human development was also discussed in this context, with reference to areas as diverse as clothing and housing, food and transport, medicine, politics, economy, science, education, and morality.
- Culture in a narrower sense: This category was initially constituted by the "fine arts" (music, painting, calligraphy, theatre, literature, film, etc.). According to Tian Rukang, culture must also be viewed as an educational subject that includes, among other things, language, normative morality and social habits (Zhu, 2006). These descriptions in turn suggest a large intersection between culture on the one hand and civilization or sophistication on the other. Nevertheless, the Chinese philosopher and historian Qian Mu tries to make a distinction in the following way: "Basically, 文明 (wen ming = civilization) and 文化 (wen hua = culture) are both related to the life of the human population. However, culture differs from civilization in that culture focuses on the outside of human life, while civilization focuses on the inside of human life. While civilization belongs to the material sector, culture belongs to the ideal sector. In this respect, civilization can spread outward, where it may find its acceptance, while culture thrives only through the internal accumulation of the spiritual characterizing a human population" (Zhu, 2006, p. 2, quoted from Hong & Shouxiang, 2009, p. 4).

According to Guo (2005), the fundamental content of culture has recently been described as a way of life, behavior and thinking. He speaks of culture as a programming of people that is controlled by their affection for one another (Hong & Shouxiang, 2009). The Chinese social scientist Li Shenzhi sees the essence of culture as providing ethical standards for human society, from which the fundamental norms governing human–nature and human–human relations emerge (Li, 1994). These modern views of culture, developed in China, are similar to Western approaches to describing and explaining culture that have emerged over the past five decades, such as those advocated by Hofstede, Trompenaars, Hall, and Thomas.

Bond (1988) reports on empirical studies that aimed to derive cross-culturally valid cultural and value dimensions using a Chinese values survey developed with Chinese colleagues working in Hong Kong (Chinese Culture Connection, 1987). For this purpose, a Chinese Value Survey (CVS) consisting of 40 items was developed and submitted to 100 respondents from 21 nations. "The scale's construction mimicked the process by which it was supposed that value surveys are typically produced, namely, that researchers mine their own cultural traditions without any regard for the traditions of other distinct groups" (Bond, 1988, p. 1010). Using a factor analysis, two factors were identified. Items with high positive loadings on Factor I express prosocial values that generally strengthen cohesion with others. Items with a high negative loading on Factor I relate in particular to loyalty to rather narrowly defined groups (especially family) with their formative habits and customs. Factor II summarizes items that express the status of individuals in a society. Factor I received the designation "Social Integration vs. Cultural Inwardness" and Factor II the designation "Reputation vs. Social Morality." Bond (1988, p. 1012) points to a large overlap of Factor I with the value areas of caring, nurturing of tradition, and conformity identified by Schwartz. For Factor II, Bond sees references to the value dimension of social power identified by Schwartz. New cultural dimensions were not identified using the Chinese Value Survey.

Based on preliminary work by the Chinese Culture Connection (1987), Fan (2000) presented a list of 71 values that he believes are shared by the Chinese population. Fan added 31 values to the 40 items in the initial list of Chinese values, citing an extensive review of publications on Chinese culture and management in China as the reason for this procedure. Fan then assigned each of the 71 values to one of eight value areas based on his personal assessment. Table 2.8 shows the list of cultural values according to Fan (2000). The authors are not aware of any empirical work based on this list of values, however.

Table 2.8: Cultural values in China according to Fan (2000, p. 13).

Cultural values in China from an inside perspective (emic-approach)

National Traits

1 Patriotism
2 A sense of cultural superiority
3 Respect for tradition
4 Bearing hardships
5 Knowledge (education)
6 Governing by leaders instead of by law
7 Equality/egalitarianism
8 Moderation, following the middle way

Interpersonal Relations

9 Trustworthiness
10 Jen-ai/Kindness (forgiveness, compassion)
11 Li/Propriety
12 People being primarily good
13 Tolerance of others
14 Harmony with others
15 Courtesy
16 Abasement/Humbleness
17 A close, intimate friend
18 Observation of rites and social rituals
19 Reciprocation of greetings, favours, and gifts
20 Repayment of both the good or the evil that another person has caused you
21 Face (protecting, giving, gaining and losing)

Family/Social Orientation

22 Filial piety
23 Chastity in women
24 Kinship
25 Veneration of the old
26 Loyalty to superiors
27 Deference to authority
28 Hierarchical relationships by status and observing this order
29 Conformity/group orientation
30 A sense of belonging
31 Reaching consensus or compromise
32 Avoiding confrontation
33 Benevolent autocrat/Paternalistic
34 Solidarity
35 Collectivism

Work Attitude

36 Industry (working hard)
37 Commitment

38 Thrift (saving)
39 Persistence (perseverance)
40 Patience
41 Prudence (carefulness)
42 Adaptability

Business Philosophy

43 Non-competition
44 Not guided by profit
45 Guanxi (personal connection or networking)
46 Attaching importance to long-lasting relationship, not gains
47 Wealth
48 Resistance to corruption
49 Being conservative
50 Morality

Personal Traits

51 Te (virtue, moral standard)
52 Sense of righteousness/Integrity
53 Sincerity
54 Having a sense of shame
55 Wisdom/Resourcefulness
56 Self-cultivation
57 Personal steadiness and stability
58 Keeping oneself disinterested and pure
59 Having few desires
60 Being gentleman anytime
61 Obiligation for one's family and nation
62 Pragmatic/to suit a situation
63 Contentedness with one's position in life

Time Orientation

64 Past-time oriented
65 Continuity/time viewed as circular rather than linear
66 Taking a long rang view

Relationship with Nature

67 The way (Tao)
68 Fatalism/Karma (believing in one's own fate)
69 Yuan
70 Harmony between man and nature
71 Unity of Yin and Yang

Trust in Chinese Culture

In Fan's overview, the value of trustworthiness can be found in the domain of interpersonal relationships. This suggests that trust in Chinese culture is of great importance in building and maintaining interpersonal relationships. But how is trust understood in Chinese culture? To this end, it is helpful to examine how the construct of trust is understood by Chinese social scientists. Linggi (2011) refers to approaches by Dong Caisheng (2005), Gao Yulin and Yang Zhou (2006) and by Lin Bin and Li Ping (2005). Linggi's remarks on these approaches are summarized below, since they offer one of the few access points to the relevant Chinese literature.

First, it should be emphasized that the following explanations reflect the views of Chinese social scientists on the trust construct. It cannot be verified here whether these views can also be found in the Chinese population. Second, the interpretations and evaluations of the approaches presented must be based essentially on the representation of the original writings by Linggi (2011), since the original texts were not available when this book was created and therefore could not be subjected to scientific verification.

Dong (2005) defines trust as the mutual expectation of the interaction partners that the respective counterpart acts according to the norms and rules of a trust system. He understands this system of trust as a system of rules and standards that has developed in the social behavior of people in a culture. Dong (2005) postulates the existence of two types of trust systems.

(1) From the traditional Chinese culture, influenced by Confucian thinking, a trust system has developed that emphasizes morality as an intrinsic system (内在制度性, *neizai zhiduxing*). According to Confucian belief, human beings are inherently good. It is the task of education to promote the good in people and to ensure personality development based on moral principles. According to this Chinese concept, trust is morally based: people whose behavior is based on morality can trust one another.

(2) In contrast, the traditional Western, Christian-influenced cultures do not emphasize the promotion of the good in people, but rather the avoidance of evil. This is done by establishing a legal system that sanctions deviant behavior. This is intended to inhibit people's inherent "tendency towards the bad" (人性, *renxing*). According to Dong (2005), law and order are the instruments of an extrinsic trust system (外在制度性, *waizai zhiduxing*).

In Dong's view, the trust systems contain control mechanisms for the purpose of maintaining trust. These mechanisms served to prevent trust from being abused. In Chinese culture, there is a soft and informal control of social interactions, the main method of which is informal punishment through moral education and instruction. As examples, Dong (2005) cites the repression, criticism or censorship by public opinion of those who have betrayed the trust of others. According to Dong (2005), in the extrinsic systems of Western cultures, social interactions are determined by formal control mechanisms. These mechanisms are designed to ensure that law and order are followed.

Dong (2005) derives the basis for interpersonal trust from the trust systems he postulates. In traditional China he sees a pattern of trust based on affection (因亲情而信, *yin qinqing er xin*); in modern Western societies, he assigns the pattern of trust based on principle (因原则而信, *yin yuanze er xin*). He sees relationships based on specific affection (especially to blood relatives, other relatives and friends) as a fundamental feature of traditional Chinese society, since people, given their very limited social mobility, lived mainly in the circle of relatives and friends (熟人, *shuren*). In contrast, in modern Western cultures, Dong sees societies of strangers (陌生人社会, *moshengren shehui*) with high social mobility and relationships based on legal principles.

Dong's line of reasoning can be summarized as follows: Dong (2005) assigns one trust system to both the traditional Chinese culture and to modern Western societies. These systems are rooted in religion and philosophy (Confucian vs. Christian) and have developed in view of the interaction partners who are particularly common (family and friends in China, strangers in Western cultures). In Linggi's (2011) description of Dong's (2005) approach, there are no references to empirical work based on Dong's considerations.

Linggi (2011) speculates that Gao and Yang (2006) responded to positions expressed by Western social scientists that contemporary Chinese society is characterized by low levels of interpersonal trust. They emphasize that in traditional Chinese society, trust (诚信, *chengxin*) is one of the central social virtues. In their descriptive approach, Gao and Yang (2006) distinguish three structural forms of social trust: chains of trust (信任链, *xinrenlian*), circles of trust (信任圈, *xinrenquan*) and trust networks (信任网, *xinrenwang*). Gao and Yang use these structural forms to compare the trust structures in Chinese society with those in Western societies.

Chains of trust serve to build trust between individuals whose social distance from one another is great and between whom direct trust-inspiring actions have therefore not yet emerged. A chain of trust can be understood here as a series of trusting relationships, which ultimately creates a multi-level bridge of trust between the previously unconnected interaction partners. A chain of trust thus depicts a relationship of trust between two actors with multi-level, linear transmission (Gao & Yang, 2006, after Linggi, 2011).

The circle of trust denotes the group within which chains of trust can be built. Because individuals can be members of different groups, circles of trust can partially overlap. Such overlaps make it easier to build relationships of trust across group boundaries. According to Gao and Yang (2006), a large number of trust chains and trust circles can combine to form a trust network.

In Chinese society, Gao and Yang (2006) see relationships of trust mainly in the form of chains and circles of trust. Trust characterizes personal or group-related relationships based on (blood) kinship, common geographical origin (cf. also Tong & Yong,

1998) or emotional affection. Therefore, in China, the group of people who are trusted is limited to certain people or groups, and interpersonal trust in a specific relationship is high. In Western societies, chains and circles of trust are of secondary importance; instead, networks of trust would emerge between individuals based on general or "public" trust based on contracts and laws. Since trust in China is essentially based on morals, habits and feelings, the risk of a loss of trust is rather high according to Gao and Yang (2006). One explanation for this could be that transgressions of moral principles are sanctioned less clearly than breaches of law and order in Western societies. For example, Bierbrauer (1992) examined how cultural background influences forms of reaction to violations of norms (see also Kam & Bond, 2009). In Western cultures, on the other hand, trust is based on institutions, law and legislation, which is why the developing trust networks are generally more stable, as Linggi (2011) concludes after reviewing the work of Gao and Yang (2006).

Gao and Yang (2006) list the degree of economic development, the prevailing social structures, a different radius of interaction when establishing interpersonal relationships, the prevailing cultural orientations in the societies and the established legal systems as causes for the different trust structures in Western societies and in Chinese society. According to Gao and Yang (2006), changes in social structures under the force of economic modernization will likely result in changes in trust structures in Chinese society going forward (see also Bond & King, 1985).

Lin and Li (2005) start their reflections with an analysis of terms used in English (trust, believe and credit) and in Chinese (*chengxin* 诚信, *xinren* 信任, *xinlai* 信赖, *xinyong* 信用) with reference to trust. Although Lin and Li (2005) see overlaps between the English and Chinese terms, they detect differences in the meaning of the individual terms. The two authors see trust in Chinese society as best expressed by the term "*chengxin*" (诚信) in the sense of sincerity and integrity, while they assume that trustworthiness (credit) is emphasized in Western societies.

Similar to Dong (2005), Lin and Li (2005) assume that there is a "predisposition" to mutual trust in Chinese society. Accordingly, individuals try to achieve moral and character perfection through correct behavior. This corresponds to the Confucian ideal of personality. Linggi (2011, p. 138) summarizes the reasoning presented by Lin and Li (2005, p. 102) as follows: "In traditional Chinese culture, trust is essentially seen as a basic evaluation standard of people and as a basic belief according to which people should be judged. It develops on the level of morality during the formation of beings."

In contrast, Lin and Li (2005) understand trust in Western cultural concepts and language systems in terms of keeping promises and returning what is borrowed. The Western concept of trust in the sense of trustworthiness (credit) is a component or prerequisite of real (economic) relationships and is reflected, for example, in contracts. Finally, Lin and Li (2005) conclude that in Western societies trust has a clear tendency towards law; in the Chinese tradition, on the other hand, sincerity (诚信, *chengxin*) constitutes the basic moral attitude of the people.

Lin and Li (2005) assign differences in the limited circles from which interaction partners for social and economic relationships could be selected as the reason for the different concepts of trust in China and in Western societies. In traditional China, such relationships were mainly limited to (blood) relatives and people with the same regional or professional affiliation due to natural economic production methods and limited mobility. The aim here was to gain trustworthiness through one's own sincerity and ultimately to gain the trust of one's interaction partners. In Western societies, the possible interaction partners were far less limited to a region dominated by family or acquaintances but had a much broader range of strangers as a basis. Lin and Li (2005) consider a mechanism to maintain trust to be essential here, which uses coercive measures on the basis of law and order to guarantee a victim the opportunity to investigate a disputed matter and, if necessary, to receive compensation (cf. Linggi, 2011, p. 139; see also Jing & Bond, 2015).

Lin and Li (2005) list three potential reasons that may have led to the emergence of different concepts of trust in China and Western societies: cultural development pathways, economic structures and religious-philosophical traditions.

– Pathways of cultural development: China's cultural development followed the path of "Asian antiquity" (亚细亚的古代, *yaxiya de gudai*), in which blood ties represent an important basis and that ultimately led from clan to nation state. Family and state showed similar structures, with the family being the foundation of the state and the state being the extension of the family. The moral principles for the family thus became the foundation for the moral code of politics, business and society. Thus, the distinction between intimates and strangers in family-level relationships was transferred to the societal level when social and economic relationships are established.

    In Western societies, cultural development took the path of "classic antiquity" (古典的古代, *gudian de gudai*), which stipulated the independence of the individual and a separation between public and private property. Interpersonal relationships were not limited to family relationships, which is why a law-based contractual relationship had to be established for them and for the relationship between the individual, society and government. These societal provisions guaranteed the legal existence and development of independent economic agents. In Western societies, according to Lin and Li (2005), these provisions have led to the development of rather higher levels of generalized trust and trust in strangers in particular (see also Jing & Bond, 2015).

– Economic structures: Economic organization in traditional China was feudal for long periods of time, with the prevailing structure of the means of production being that of small farmers and agriculture. Farm land was predominantly cultivated in collectives, social mobility was restricted and individuals were dependent on blood relatives or regional communities for guiding their decisions and actions. Neither the social relationships nor the developing personalities would have reached a level of development in which a contract culture with equality as a prerequisite for a credit system could have been established for the management of commodities exchange.

In Western societies, economic relations at first nationally, and later internationally, expanded continuously and at increasing speed. Contracts as a legal transfer medium have gained in importance and, together with a functioning credit system, have formed the framework for successful economic relationships. "The Western concept of trust emphasized . . . on the one hand the development towards credit, which was guaranteed by laws, on the other hand the generalized trust towards strangers determined to a certain extent the economic structure of Western society and its development" (Linggi, 2011, pp. 141ff.).

–   Religious-philosophical traditions: According to Lin and Li (2005), Confucianism, as the official orthodox tradition of the Chinese Empire, demanded morality as the basis for social relationships and promoted the character ideal of the virtuous nobleman who constantly improves his behavior through continuous self-perfection. He posited the achievement of an ideal society through practicing sincerity in all social relationships. According to Lin and Li (2005), however, with the entry of Chinese society into the age of the market economy, the lack of a protective mechanism against moral risks ((道德奉献, *daode fengxian*) became apparent "because there was no institution that could have ensured and protected the promised credits" (Linggi, 2011, p. 142).

Traditional Western societies are characterized by a religious tradition in which all people are allowed to feel like children of God and have the sacred duty to be industrious and frugal. Reformation and Enlightenment would have led to the development of rational methods of analysis and to an awareness of the rule of law for social order and administration. An individualism that emphasized the equality and freedom of the individual, the striving for individual benefit and the satisfaction of needs and at the same time demanded responsibility towards society had developed. However, since man was recognized as inherently bad-tempered, agreements of credit and trust had to be institutionally and legally supported, for they could not rely on individual sincerity alone.

Against this background, Lin and Li (2005) claim that in China, with its entry into a global market with its complex economic relationships among multiple players, changes in society, and in particular with regard to the prevailing concept of trust, must take place, so that the country and society are able to cope with and benefit from the challenges of modernization.

Conclusion

A review of numerous empirical studies from the late 1990s has shown that the success of international joint ventures is influenced to a considerable extent by the way in which the cultural differences of the employees are managed. At the same time, interpersonal trust has come into focus as one determinant of the success of international economic cooperation. With a few exceptions (e.g., Johnson et al., 1996; Krishnan, Martin & Noorderhaven, 2006), most empirical studies have examined the importance of trust for the success of joint ventures in relatively homogeneous cultures. Given the growth and intensity of international and intercultural economic cooperation, the question arises as to whether and to what extent the processes that lead to mutual trust between the actors depend upon their cultural orientations.

In this study, trust in intercultural joint ventures is the focus of examination. The assessments and perceptions of decision-makers from two cultural areas are to be compared: Germany and the People's Republic of China (PRC). These cultural areas were chosen because joint ventures between Chinese and German companies have been entered into in large numbers in recent decades and are likely to continue in the future.

3 Confucianism, Daoism and Buddhism and Their Influence on Chinese Culture

In the last chapter, we suggested a profile of Chinese culture on the basis of the respective cultural theories. From a culture-historical perspective, China's cultural sphere has evolved over a development that has lasted more than 5,000 years. Among the major influential factors that have shaped Chinese culture are Confucianism, Daoism and Buddhism. In the following, the constitutive characteristics of these world views will be presented. Specific examples will show how they are reflected nowadays in daily Chinese life.

Confucianism

> 安分守己 – *Follow the rules and be modest.* (Confucian proverb)

Life and Teachings of Confucius

The term "Confucianism" stands for a world view developed by a Chinese thinker who lived in the fifth century BC Confucianism is regarded "as one of the main trends (三教) in Chinese intellectual history" (Woesler, 2010, p. 21). The school named after Confucius offered an "ethically justified response to the question concerning the meaning of life and the social order" (Küng & Ching, 1988, p. 94). In Chinese, Confucianism is denoted as "儒学 (*ru xue,* school of the meek)." This denotation suggests a fundamental humanist attitude that portrays a constituent feature of the Confucian philosophy (Küng & Ching, 1988, p. 89). Its overriding goal is to blend in with the world and not to detach from the world (Schluchter, 1983, p. 36). Confucius' work does not cater to a transcendental perspective; it is geared towards life in this world. As a consequence, Confucianism should not be regarded as a religious, but rather an ideological system.

Confucius was born in 551 BC, the son of an impoverished aristocrat in the Lu Commandery, around the same time as Buddha in India and Socrates in Greece. Now situated in the province of Shandong, the Lu Commandery of the time formed part of the Zhou Dynasty when Confucius was alive. Though this dynasty had ruled China since the 11th century (up to 256 BC), it had continued to diminish in significance due to various internal and external armed conflicts (Schmidt-Glintzer, 2008). The downfall of the Zhou Dynasty is defined by deep-rooted social upheavals as well as the depletion of traditional norms and values. The "crisis of passed-down morality" (Roetz,

https://doi.org/10.1515/9783111344560-003

1995, p. 46) triggered by this decline is a central theme of the conversations that Confucius conducted with his students (Wilhelm, 1989; hereinafter simply referred to as the "Analects").

During the course of the changes that occurred within society in the Zhou Dynasty, the position of the nobility continued to wane. That someone was born into nobility ceased to become a guarantee for their gaining employment at the royal courts. Holding public office became a matter of the qualifications held by the individual in question: "In teaching, there should be no division of class" (Analects 15.38). Educational measures aimed, on the one hand, at forming the moral integrity of the individual's personality while, on the other, forming a professional work ethic. This training occurred in the schools attended by nobility or was performed by private tutors.

Confucius was such a freelance teacher. Of all the various roles attributed to him, that of the *pedagogue* was the most important role. Confucius' "initial motivation lay . . . in convincing others of the need to learn in the first place" (van Ess, 2009, p. 19). Confucius believed in the power and joy of learning: "Learning and constantly practicing that which is learned – is this not also a source of joy?" (Analects I.1). It would be reasonable to assume that this impulse was the reason why the learning process is held in such high esteem at the beginning of the "Analects." Confucius perceived himself not only as a teacher who propagated the principle of lifelong learning but also as a learner: "Whenever I was with one or two others, my teacher was always present" (Analects 7.1.).

In Confucian education, Roetz (1995) sees a harbinger of the meritocracy and advancement society that came into being in 20th-century China following the fall of Imperial China. In its aftermath, the much-vaunted studiousness of many Chinese found its roots in clearly Confucian approaches.

According to Confucius, the primary task of a teacher is to convey to their students – as they prepare for the life ahead of them – the "right" ethics, i.e., a set of values that acts as a "compass" showing the right lifepath forwards. He includes in his teachings the values and norms of Ancient China. In doing so, Confucius shows himself to be a traditionalist rather than an innovator: "I only transmit and never create anything new" (Analects 7.1).

Confucius spent many years crossing those principalities that had increased their autonomy during the slow but sure demise of the Zhou Dynasty. During this time he was not only engaged in teaching but also advised the princes who were subservient to the Zhou state. Throughout his life, Confucius never took on an executive post. This is where a further role that has also been attributed to Confucius comes to light: That of a *politician* contemplating a virtuous form of leadership of a state and society and attempting to bring these thoughts to the fore as a political adviser.

The art of ruling entails having each holder of a leadership position being assigned a specific role: "The prince is a prince, the public servant a public servant, the father a father, the son a son" (Analects 12.11). If each of them fulfils a designated role, then the state itself will function in harmony. This is true of everyone serving the state, whether low-level public servants or rulers. At the same time, particular duties are imposed on the dignitaries at the upper echelons of the state. They are required to avail of the "right" ethos, i.e., be familiar with and implement the established laws and customs. "He did nothing and all was well ordered (in the empire), that was Shun. What did he do? He simply composed himself with reverence and sat facing due south, nothing more!" (Analects 15.4). If rulers follow the art of ruling and are virtuous in doing so, then the populace will be satisfied: "Good governance makes those nearby happy and attracts those from afar" (Analects 13.16).

At the same time, the governing individual has a particular duty to lead by example. On this matter, Confucius is believed to have said: "If the superiors were without desires, the subordinates would not steal either, even if they were paid to do so" (Do-Dinh, 1987, p. 72). Paternalistic leadership is regarded as a leadership principle of Confucianism (Chen & Lee, 2008, p. 171 ff.): "The ruler is strict but benevolent at the same time" (Chen, n.d.). According to Confucius, the ruler should lead their people as a father would his family: with benevolence, but with a strict hand at the same time. Unlike the so-called "authoritarian leadership" model, with its unilateral orientation on the imposition of the will of the leader, the needs and wishes of those being led are to be taken on board in a patriarchal leadership style. Confucius' leadership doctrine, which also focuses on human goodness, is an expression of Confucius' humanistic philosophy. Do-Dinh (1987, p. 97) even goes so far as to believe that it is possible to perceive harbingers of a "democratic spirit" in the government policy of "benevolence, virtue and tolerance" propagated by Confucius to which the populace will also be attached.

The third role that can be attributed to Confucius is that of a sociologist. The social world, in all its manifestations, is a particular focus of his attention. A constitutive feature of Confucian thinking is its strong hierarchical orientation. Power within the state and society is divided unequally; there is a wide hierarchical divide within each of the individual social units. Social stratification is based on superior–subordinate relationships.

Confucian thought holds the hierarchical set-up of society to be a prerequisite for peaceful co-existence within society. The individual is required to fit in to the social fabric without objection. "That no individual . . . would rebel against the superior, that is seldom" (Analects 1.2). The hierarchical set-up of society orders social relationships and is the prerequisite for harmonious co-existence; maintaining a harmonious society requires that each individual fulfills the obligations associated with their relative status. These especially include obligations toward one's family, society, friends and the state. At the same time, the individuals constituting these social units are always seen in terms of their mutual relationship.

Including the individual in the collective does not mean, however, that people need to remain for the rest of their lives within their social class or group into which they were born. Confucius' world view asserts the possibility of social advancement, in particular through learning. This social mobility model found its expression in the qualification system at the Chinese imperial court that gave every individual – irrespective of their social background – the opportunity to work their way up the hierarchical system. The principle of individual advancement through studiousness and examinations continues to apply in modern-day China (see also King & Bond, 1985).

Aside from its pedagogical and political discussions, the legacy of Confucius also concerns behavioral ethics. In this context, he shows himself to be a philosopher, who, through his guiding principles, developed "general principles of action" (Waley, 1938, p. 55) that work toward a peaceful and harmonious co-existence of individuals with one another and the state.

At the core of his structure of value and norms are five virtues (Do-Dinh, 1987, p. 87):

仁 (ren) – Benevolence
义 (yi) – Righteousness
礼 (li) – Propriety, i.e. the upholding of social norms and rituals
智 (zhi) – Wisdom
信 (xin) – Trustworthiness

In terms of their ranking within the system of humanist values of Confucianism, *"benevolence" (ren)* is paramount. A look at the pictogram for *ren* (仁) offers a deep insight into Chinese thinking: It contains the characters for "human being" (人) and "two" (二). The human being is not perceived as an individual but rather as someone within a community and in reciprocity with another individual. This view reveals the collectivist principles underlying the world view of Confucianism.

Generally speaking, *ren* means "love for the individual" (Analects 12.22), i.e., in terms of benevolent love and care (Roetz, 1995, p. 69). But *ren* also means being pleasantly taken by the other with all one's heart (Roetz, 1995, p. 69). *Ren* is also interpreted as "humanity in all its richness and perfection" (Do-Dinh, 1987, p. 88). Given the ambiguity of the Chinese language, *ren* can additionally be comprehended as respecting the other individual as a being "just like I am" or, in short, "fairness" (Roetz, 1995, p. 71).

Benevolence, as perceived by Confucius, is founded on the principle of mutuality. This is denoted as the Golden Rule: "Do not do unto others what you would not want them to do to you" (Analects 15.23). This behavioral maxim can also be found in the New Testament: "In everything, then, do to others as you would have them do to you" (Matthew 7.12). Under the principle of reciprocity or mutuality, the individual grants to others what they would want for themselves. From a psychological perspective, a mental swapping of roles thus takes place whereby one person views themselves from the perspective of the other or puts themselves in the position of the other (cf. Roetz, 1995, p. 73).

The fundamental concepts of the Golden Rule are deeply entrenched in numerous cultures across the globe. It is one of those fundamental values which apply interculturally and thus form an integral part of a global ethic that links world cultures (Küng, 1992).

In the canon of Confucian virtues, "Propriety" *(li)* also takes on great importance. Propriety and the rituals on which this is founded are "the epitome of the well-mannered decency of sophisticated etiquette. Differentiated by rank and role, age and gender" (Roetz, 1995, p. 46). The rituals are binding behavioral norms that regulate every ordinary and extraordinary matter of life down to the very last detail. These include marriage, sacrifices, clothing, eating, and burial and bereavement ceremonies. The rituals provide the individual with near-seamless guidance in every aspect of life. In the words of Confucius: "Those who do not learn the Li are without solid standing" (Analects 16.13).

The canon of values of Confucianism is supplemented by a series of social duties (Woesler, 2010, p. 23) that the individual is required to fulfill if they wish to lead a virtuous and responsible-minded life. These include "filial duty" or piety (孝, *xiao)*, which traditionally play a special role in the Chinese social system. The duty to treat one's parents with reverence holds true even after death: as an expression of his piety, the son was required to observe three years of mourning upon the death of his father.

The "Doctrine of the Mean" (中庸, *zhong yong*) represents a further fundamental concept of Chinese thinking that is closely associated with Confucianism. Maintaining the middle way means that "associating with extremes can only bring harm" (Analects 2.16). "Those who adhere to the mean as a general guide can preserve their bodies, lead a fulfilled life, care for their family, and savour life in advanced years" (Zhuangzi, Chapter 3.1; in Kalinke, 2019, p. 37). Confucius is not encouraging an adjusted mean here but rather the imperative of restraint and of balance in a variety of action alternatives and role commitments. When Confucius says: "Stay faithful to the mean" (Analects 20.1), this means: "no excessiveness, no direct partisanship; equanimity and harmony" (Do-Dinh, 1987, p. 127) or a balancing of values (Roetz, 1995, p. 91).

The values and norms of Confucianism are embodied ideal-typically in the "Analects" through the so-called *Noble One* (君子, Junzi). The Noble One is diligent and learns from the past: "I am not born with knowledge. I love the old and am keen in my endeavours" (Analects 7.19). Irrespective of his social background, the Noble One is proud, modest and peaceable. "A noble one has his pride but never argues" (Analects 15.22). Toward his ruler, the Noble One displays loyalty but does not subordinate himself like a slave. He is equally not reliant on how his social environment perceives him: "Do not grumble when the others misjudge you – is that not noble?" (Analects 1.1).

The Noble One does not aspire to material goods and advancement. He heeds the virtues and customs and takes on the tasks facing him: "When the noble one assumes an office, he fulfils his duty" (Analects 18.7). His actions and deeds always revolve around the imperative of benevolence. Self-examination, self-awareness, self-empowerment and self-esteem all form part of his individual personality. The individual's uppermost development goal is to "cultivate the Self" through a "responsible-minded assumption of social duties in moral integrity" (Roetz, 1995, p. 87). For Confucius, the evolution and strengthening of the self is the focal point of personality development: "The way of the Noble One is founded on the Self" (Zhongyong 29, in Roetz, 1995, p. 80). This realization evokes memories of Goethe's saying: "The greatest happiness for children of the earth is only personality" (Goethe, 2013, p. 65).

Through his Confucian-influenced attitude and conduct, the Noble One takes on the function of a role model for those who interact with him: "The Noble One resembles the Pole Star: he dwells at his location with all of the stars orbiting around him" (Analects 2,1).

By placing the "personal self-unfolding" (Scharmann & Roth, 1976, p. 3) of the Noble One at the centre of contemporary considerations in developmental psychology, Confucius is drawing closer to an educative ideal that is characteristic of occidental individualism. Its maxim is: "Know who you are and be yourself" – a demand that could also have been uttered by Confucius. Against this backdrop, Confucius should not only be understood as a proponent of a collectivist worldview. Instead, when appraising Confucius, a differentiated perspective would appear more appropriate that also considers the individualistic component of his work.

Confucianism in Modern-day China

In the aftermath of Confucius' death, his teachings have profoundly influenced Chinese culture for more than 2,500 years. To this day, his thinking about people in their social entanglements continues to form an integral part of Chinese society and thinking. This is evidenced in various studies conducted by cultural researchers (Chinese Culture Connection, 1987; Hofstede, 2001; House et al., 2004).

The "Doctrine of the Mean" thus continues to be a guiding principle for behavior in everyday Chinese life even today, and especially as a principle of balance in a "culture of blandness": "Depending on the type of bland taste, whose merit it is to remain less precise and thus always adaptable, the motif of blandness is able to renew itself in Chinese culture" (Jullien, 1999, p. 9). The blandness motif also dictates people's eating and drinking habits (e.g., by preferring (luke)warm over hot dishes and teas). A further example of the continuing applicability of Confucian thinking is apparent in the Chinese Party's emphasis on "social harmony" as a primary value and thus how it draws on notions that Confucius held in high esteem 2,000 years ago (see Bond, 1986).

Collectivist and hierarchical concepts, i.e., the characteristically Confucian body of thought, are also noticeable in Chinese business life and, as always, dictate the attitudes and conduct of the Chinese in a business context: in Chinese cultural circles, management is primarily viewed to mean leading groups, i.e., is thus dictated by collectivism (Leung, 2012). There, the sense of company solidarity plays a completely different role from that in the Western hemisphere. The principle of hierarchy impacts how business entities are set up and function. The style of management and communication practiced there is primarily "top-down", in keeping with the paternalistic leadership model (Fischer, 2012).

Through its collectivist and hierarchical economic system, modern-day China has grown to become a successful industrial nation since Mao's death. The successful abatement of life-threatening poverty can be seen as one of its greatest achievements. The elimination of corruption, which also frequently goes hand in glove with collectivist, hierarchical economic systems, continues to pose a great challenge, however (Wuttke, 2012).

Daoism

顺其自然 – *Let nature take its course.* (Daoist adage)

The Teachings of Daoism

Daoism denotes a worldview, the establishment of which is attributed to the legendary Laozi (i.e., the "Old Master"). In many aspects, Daoism represents a contrast to the teachings of Confucius. While Confucius can be regarded first and foremost as a social philosopher, Laozi can be viewed primarily as a natural philosopher. To Confucius, humankind as a social being forms the main focus of his attention, whereby Laozi is, above all, concerned with the relationship between humankind and nature. Daoism also surfaces as a religion, however, whereby its followers believe in an invisible world beyond this life (Küng & Ching, 1988).

As outlined above, Confucian thought is associated with notions such as collectivism, hierarchy, harmony and order; it is based on a more static worldview. By contrast, Daoism tends to be more individualistic and less hierarchical; it regards all things as being linked to one another and undergoing permanent change: everything is in flux (*Daodejing*, Chapter 25; in Simon, 2009). The symbolism of water takes on particular significance here.

In Chinese history, Laozi takes on a wide variety of roles – as a teacher, philosopher, even going as far as being a god-like being. Much like Confucianism, the historical backdrop to the teachings of Daoism can be found in the Zhou Dynasty (11th century–256 BC). Probably no such person called Laozi ever existed. The legend, however, recounts a wandering scholar who is said to have lived at the same time as Confucius and in the Lu Commandery (approximately 500 BC). He carved out an existence as an archivist, teacher and adviser. The legend also claims that Laozi headed west (i.e., to India) towards the end of his life. It is during a respite at a border crossing that he is said to have written his famous work, "Daodejing." This work has established his reputation as one of the great Chinese philosophers.

The Daodejing is a slim volume that, among other things, bears the additional title "The Scripture of the Way and its Power" (Simon, 2009). The work largely covers the following topics (cf. Kalinke, 2011):

- The status of humankind in nature and the universe
- The way to wisdom
- The art of governing

The 81 chapters encompassing the writings attributed to Laozi have no progressive, systematic train of thought. They represent a collection of aphorisms whose origins date back as far as the 5th century BC. Over the course of time, several text versions and comments have emerged that, though attributed to Laozi, are, at times, contradictory. A common thread is discernible in numerous versions, however, as are pertinent commonalities. Centuries-old manuscripts are repeatedly found – typically as grave goods – which provide new impetus for Laozi researchers.

The focal point of Daodejing is the *dao* (道) as a central concept. In keeping with traditional Chinese thought, at no point in the text is a definition given as to what the term, *dao*, should signify. The *dao* of Laozi is seen as the way, road, course of events, way out, purpose, divine reason, law of nature or even "a guiding way" (Hansen, 1983, p. 229). This way (*dao*) is not a straight, continuous way, however; instead, it can be perceived as a "guiding path" (Kalinke, 2011, p. 64). Just as is the case with nature, the way of *dao* cannot be pre-determined. This unsettled state and unpredictability comprise one of its key features. And since *dao* is constantly undergoing change, it essentially cannot be named for what it is. "I know not its name; assign it a name; that name shall be *dao*" (*Daodejing*, Chapter 25; in Simon, 2009, p. 85).

In their work on Daoism, Schipper, Girardot and Duval (1993, p. 3) provide a more in-depth definition of how the term *dao* can be interpreted: "The first meaning of the character *dao* is 'way': something underlying the change and transformation of all things, the spontaneous process regulating the natural cycle of the universe. It is in this process, along this way, that the world as we see it, is the creation of which we are an integral part, finds its unity." According to Daoism, *dao* existed before the world came into being and is the primordial basis of the world: "A thing exists, grown from the flow of chaos, born before heaven and earth. Inaudible, oh, empty, oh, alone it stands upright without ever changing; it is active across its entire radius and never runs into danger. It can be called the mother of that which is found below heaven" (*Daodejing*, Chapter 25; in Simon, 2009, p. 85).

Accordingly, *dao* can be regarded as being a higher-order power, as the supreme reality, as the absolute that ranks above all phenomena and precedes the universe: *dao* is the primordial basis of all phenomena, the mother of the world (Darga, 2003, p. 60). The nature, being and effect of *dao* can be illustrated using the imagery of a storm sweeping across a landscape and leaving behind chaos and destruction. It is thus more than a singular act of creation or big bang that triggered the world into evolution. *Dao* is rather a constant intrinsic presence in nature, everywhere; it "lives" in all things and all processes. As such, all phenomena in the world are interlinked and/or networked. Wherever *dao* is allowed to take effect, Daoist thinking asserts that things develop through a natural process. Accordingly, no attempts should be undertaken to accelerate the natural development process or to guide it in a different direction.

In Daoism and the Chinese world view, the conceptual pairing of yin and yang takes on central significance. As far back as the 1st century BC, corresponding characters appeared on bronze inscriptions. In them, the word *yin* stands for the shaded northern slope of a mountain, for darkness and rainclouds. *Yang* stands for the sunny southern slope of a mountain, for light and sunshine. As of the 4th century, *yin* and *yang* were regarded as symbols of vital energy and drawn upon to explain natural phenomena. Accordingly, *yin* is attributed to the cold, wet and soft materials, calm and of the earth, while *yang* stands for warmth, the solid, spiritual, movement, and the heavens; the female counterpart to the *yin*, the male principle is attributed to the *yang*.

The famous *yin–yang* symbol (see Figure 3.1) has been around since the 13th century. It symbolizes the simultaneous, complementary, indivisible nature of the two primordial forces, but also their variable influence at any given moment. According to Wang (2012, p. 5), the *yin–yang* symbol represents a paradigm (Kuhn, 1970), i.e., a fundamental school of thought based on which all phenomena in the cosmos are interdependently linked and mutually affect one another.

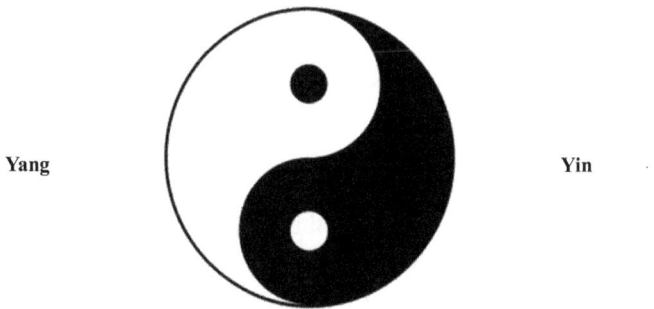

Yang   Yin

Yin (the female principle) = the cold, soft, material, calm and the earth

Yang (the male principle) = warmth, the solid, spiritual, movement and heaven

Figure 3.1: *Yin–yang* symbol. *Yin* and *yang* as an expression of the simultaneous existence of opposites that are joined to form a harmonious whole ("Both/And Principle"). Adapted from Darga (2003, p. 36).

Yin and *yang* are fed from the same source and regarded as differing manifestations of being. They are inter-related: the impact of the male principle can only be seen in conjunction with the impact of the female process – just like any coin has two sides that are reciprocally related. In much the same way as the left and the right hand complement each other, so, too, can the respective functions of the sympathetic and parasympathetic nervous systems only be understood in terms of their antithesis. Here, Darga (2003, p. 36) refers to the *yin–yang* relationship as a "dynamic polarity."

In the opinion of Daoists, dynamic polarity is a key principle underlying the design of the cosmos and the world. The simultaneous existence of complementary occurrences and/or the evolutionary succession of complementary occurrences is a defining principle of ancient Chinese thought. The notion of a unit of contrasting pairs that can only be meaningfully conceived in terms of their reciprocal interrelatedness can also be denoted as holistic, integrated thinking. This principle constitutes the basis of contemporary cross-cultural psychological research on dialectical thinking (see, e.g., Peng, Spencer-Rodgers & Zhong 2006).

To facilitate the theoretical penetration of the *yin–yang* concept, Wang (2012, p. 3) has designed a framework into which its constitutive elements can be categorized: "First, yinyang describes a condition in which there exist two opposite but related and interdependent ideas or objects. Second, yinyang offers a normative model with balance, harmony and sustainability as ideals. Third, a more scholarly understanding involves a conceptual construction, whereby yinyang is characterized as a 'correlative' mode of thought or cosmology."

The *yin–yang* symbol reflects the world of ideas that interfaces with the *yin–yang* philosophy: one of the key elements of Daoist thought concerns the permanent change and alteration of events in the cosmos and the world. This, too, is represented symbolically by the yin–yang symbol. Louis (2003, p. 175) describes this dynamic in vivid terms: "Its two curved, interlocking geometric shapes depict a rotating, self-creating cycle of complementary opposites, of mutually dependent entities." Accordingly, the two tear-shaped elements of the *yin* and *yang* are not to be viewed as two separate entities juxtaposed mechanically with no relation to one another. Instead, they are enveloped, are inextricably conjoined, flow into and rotate around each other, impact upon one another, and create something new and perfect in and of itself by virtue of their mutual connectedness, namely a circle. In turn, the circle stands for a unit, for the whole, from which *dao* was originally sprung from the yin and yang.

Even today, Chinese thought is very profoundly influenced by Daoist thought and thus the conceptual world of the yin and yang. Traditional occidental thought leans towards clear, at times, often incontrovertible thought patterns as well as principles: A or B; black or white. Coupled with this, an attempt is often made to cling to principles once they are held to be right. Given the country's heavily context-oriented tradition of thought, people in China tend to be more prepared to take the B into consideration as a complementary perspective to the A – in keeping with the motto: The opposite is also true. "The Daoist nestles into the situation" (Kalinke, 2011, p. 186).

This contrast in thinking patterns is revealed in recent cross-cultural comparisons of analytic versus holistic styles of thinking (Nisbett et al., 2001). Instead of rigidly clinging to principles and standards believed to be right once they have been established, a trait particularly found among Germans, Chinese thinking and deeds adopt a more flexible and inclusive approach, regarded as more pragmatic.

A further guiding principle derived from Daoism is action through inaction (无为, *wu wei)*: "This is why the complete individual says: I do not engage, and still the people transform on their own. I love the silence, and still the people line up on their own; I give no instructions, and still the people are happy of their own accord" (Daodejing, Chapter 57; in Simon, 2009, p. 177). According to the Daodejing, it is the task of the ruler to broker between nature (heaven and earth) and human society. At the heart of the art of ruling stands a minimalist government policy: the ruler allows others to lead and is mindful about personally meddling in the course of events. Action through inaction (无为, *wu wei)* – this is the Daoist guiding principle for good governance.

Inactivity as a maxim does not, however, signify complete inaction. First and foremost, *wu wei* involves closely observing nature. At the same time, the Daoist assumes that things develop in spontaneous, self-organizing ways for the benefit of the whole. If it is determined, however, that a development is not working for the benefit of the whole, i.e., is not functional, then it can be brought back onto the right track with minimal intervention.

Action through inaction stands out for its:
- respect of things and people as well as the nature that is intrinsic to them
- knowledge of the natural paths of development and/or the functional course of a development
- use of opportunities to steer the natural course of developments through minimal intervention, without disrupting such a course

Effortless action thus requires the mindfulness of human beings towards their social and natural environment. This mindfulness exists in the perception of the subtleties of nature: "How the fish jump up and frolic – this is the joy of the fishes" (Zhuangzi, Chapter 17.13; in Kalinke, 2019, p. 190).

Mindfulness in general can be understood to mean mindfulness of the internal state of mind, mindfulness of the outward situation, mindfulness of the impact of one's own actions, mindfulness of the state of mind of others as well as mindfulness of nature. For, "Heaven and earth are born together with me, and the myriad things and I are one" (天地與我並生,而萬物與我為一。) So, the concept of mindfulness in Daoism entails the "practice of the Eightfold Path" (Kalinke, 2011, p. 136) covering the following elements:
1. Achieve well-being through thoughtfulness.
2. Replace thinking with silence, and complacency with the openness of the mind.
3. Place yourself in a state of indifference and sober clarity.
4. Replace feelings of happiness and pain with equanimity and collect yourself.

5. Disband the perception of specific forms and shapes and experience the infinity of space.
6. Open yourself to the boundlessness of consciousness.
7. Guide your consciousness into the sphere of non-being.
8. In the sphere of nothingness dwells your consciousness in a state of neither perceiving nor not perceiving. (Kalinke, 2011, p. 136)

Developing a mindful lifestyle is a core element of self-cultivation in the Daoist sense, i.e., the development of one's ego in keeping with the Daoist ideals of modesty, humbleness, benevolence and nature-connectedness. Longevity, as a vital life maxim of Daoism, can also only be achieved through mindfulness of oneself and all of nature.

According to Laozi, the state of conscious mindfulness is only considered to be achievable if the individual is capable of and willing to commit to self-sacrifice. Only when one succeeds in casting away everything that is of personal importance will it be possible to see oneself as being in the flow of things rather than as the focal point – only then will it be possible to appreciate things for themselves in their respective context. A wise ruler is therefore obliged to respond with mindfulness and to show consistent restraint in everything he does. He should be unselfish and leave it up to the populace to organize itself: "The ruler leaves the micro-cosmos for the people so as to secure the macro-cosmos for himself within the ritual" (Kalinke, 2011, p. 144).

A further trait held by the wise ruler is peacefulness. Any form of militarism is alien to the wise ruler of the state that lives in harmony with people-in-nature: "Good weapons are the tools of doom [.] Most beings abhor them [.] Therefore: Those with *dao* do not handle them" (Daodejing, Chapter 31; in Kalinke, 2015, p. 48). A wise, peace-loving ruler keeps the populace satisfied. His unselfish nature makes him a role model and his position at the top of the social hierarchy is accepted.

Chinese history has repeatedly seen rulers attempt to implement a Daoist government policy, e.g., during the Tang Dynasty (618–907 AD), the heyday of Chinese culture. At the same time, respect for the individual (as a part of nature) and their freedom as well as fully fledged pacifism formed the core elements of a Daoist form of governance. The benevolence of the rulers adhering to Daoism also found its expression in their rejection of the death penalty (Kalinke, 2011, p. 143).

Much like Confucianism, Daoism also entails morals and values from which interpersonal behavior and conduct follow, i.e., integrity, benevolence, justice and decency. Unlike Confucianism, these concepts of morality and value in Daoism apply solely as secondary virtues that act as behavior regulators in the social context. At the heart of the Daoist value system stands the *dao* as the core ethical principle: "should the *dao* be lost, the virtue shall follow [;] should the virtue be lost, benevolence shall follow[;] should benevolence be lost, justice shall follow[;] should justice be lost, the custom shall follow" (Daodejing, Chapter 38; in Kalinke, 2015, p. 55).

As an alternative to the Confucian-influenced virtue doctrine, Daoism demands a primal, unreflective, intuitively self-evident virtuousness, i.e., a doctrine of virtue completely devoid of moral reproach. Follow the *dao*: that is the supreme Daoist maxim for action. At the same time, the actions undertaken by the individual are not so much assessed by what is advantageous for the individual but rather what is beneficial for the whole.

From a Daoist perspective, people are neither good nor evil, because, like everything in nature, they are permeated with the *dao*. As the true one, the *dao* is value neutral. It is implicitly included in every situation facing the individual. Daoism thus does not formulate any cross-situational, transcendental principles, since these cannot do justice to the diverse nature of the world and its state of permanent change: "Human, be natural, for you are nature" (Kalinke, 2011, p. 169). This is how Kalinke phrases the ethical imperative of Daoism, which forgoes any moral demands. As previously mentioned, the primacy of the situation applies in Daoist ethics. Acting ethically within the meaning of Daoism thus entails reconciling one's own *dao* (i.e., the self) with the *dao* of the situation (i.e., its specific circumstances).

Daoism in Modern-day China

More than 2,500 years have passed since Daoism was originated in China. During this time, the Daoist world view has grown to become one of the main pillars of Chinese philosophy, which, even today, continues to "live and blossom" (van Ess, 2011, p. 116). The school of Daoism has also given rise to a secular movement with a sphere of influence that, today, extends as far as the USA (Kohn, 2004, p. 199).

Daoism has enriched Chinese culture (e.g., in painting, literature, acting) in a multitude of ways. Daily and business culture in modern-day China is clearly influenced by Daoism, as can be seen in the proverbial flexibility of many Chinese, for example. This is a constituent feature of Chinese business culture. Especially the Germans working in China, with their purported love of laws and structure, at times find it difficult to adjust to the rapid changeability with which they are frequently confronted there. Agreements and contracts lack the same binding character there that they are afforded in Germany. Unlike the norm that applies in the West: "pacta servanda sunt" (agreements must be kept), the Chinese understanding of contracts is that they can be subsequently modified and amended to suit a new situation.

A management theory has also arisen from the Daoist maxims, namely the "water-like leadership style." Unlike the paternalistic leadership theory influenced by Confucianism, this leadership style has its origins in present-day management theorizing: For Daoism, water symbolizes altruism, modesty, flexibility and transparency. Behind this is the central demand of Daoism for people to adapt to nature and align themselves to its laws. "Water-like management" is based on these same features and generates a heavily employee-oriented leadership model (Dimovski et al., 2013) that brings to mind the concepts and processes of "servant leadership" (Fischer et al., 2019). The current scientific discussion of the *"wu wei* principle" (the principle of action through inaction, Slingerland and Kleinschmidt (2014) reveal that significance continues to be bestowed on the Daoist body of thought today, including in the Western hemisphere.

The health-related behavior practiced by many Chinese also continues to be influenced by the principles of Daoism. The search for eternal life, as it applies in traditional Daoism, no longer takes center stage; it has been supplanted by caring for one's health in terms of prevention by taking precautions. This includes careful observation of one's own body.

Daoist influences are also visible in its profound connection with nature and, by the same token, with the environment. This is also reflected in the often-fierce reactions to the state's incursions into nature. Corresponding protests repeatedly flare up even though the protesters can expect to be hit with severe penalties. *Feng shui* (风水, wind and water) concerns, as in the spatial arrangement of houses, rooms and furniture to ward off evil forces, continues to be deeply rooted in Chinese thought and has also gained a broad following in the West.

The meditation, breathing, movement and combat techniques of *Qigong* (气功, "energy exercises"), with its flowing motions, which can be observed every morning in urban parks and squares, also have their origins in Daoism. When the protagonists in historical films elegantly and effortlessly float in mid-air wholly detached from any laws of gravity (as in the case of the famous blockbuster movie *Tiger and Dragon*), then factors of the Daoist body of thought are also at play. So, "Daoism continues to be a philosophical doctrine that prefers the soft to the hard, the weak to the strong and inaction to action" (van Ess, 2011, p. 115). These phenomena, which have become a part of today's everyday life, embody a particular approach that "will also take on a major role in the future" (van Ess, 2011, p. 116).

Buddhism

无欲无求 – *Renounce abundance and desire.* (Buddhist adage)

Buddhism in China

Unlike Daoism and Confucianism, Buddhism has its origins in India. In terms of its fundamental features, Chinese Buddhism resembles Indian-style Buddhism. Differences exist with regard to the rituals and practices, but less so with the dogmas. Buddhism can be differentiated from numerous non-Indian religions in "that it does not expect the redemption of people from the barriers of finiteness to result from divine grace but rather from redemption that each person seeking salvation needs to gain themselves" (von Glasenapp, 1978, n. p.).

The Buddhist faith, which reached China in the middle of the first century BC as a foreign religion (Küng & Ching, 1988), has spread across China in the course of a centuries-long process of adjustment. The integration of the Buddhist world view into Chinese culture which occurred at the same time exhibits, at times, symbiotic traits: "Was China conquered by Buddhism or, vice-versa, did China conquer Buddhism?" (Küng & Ching, 1988, S. 226). Even though Buddhism has increasingly developed into a Chinese religion in the course of history, its Indian origins are unmistakeable. These include the notion of transmigration and rebirth, which form a core element of India's religious culture and have found their way into China's religious culture through Buddhism. Over its more than 2,000-year history, the Buddhist religion has accounted for a significant portion of the Chinese population across large areas of China.

However, it has never become a religion endorsed by the state (Schmidt-Glintzer, 2005). Nonetheless, the Chinese state has sought, on numerous occasions, to legitimize its existence through the teachings of Buddhism. Such endeavours were particularly apparent during the Tang Dynasty (617–907 BC) when Chinese Buddhism reached its pinnacle (Cheng, 2022). Similar attempts occurred during the Qing Dynasty (1644–1911 AD) under the foreign rule of the Manchus, who came from the north to conquer the Chinese empire (Elverskog, 2006).

Since the era of the Tang Dynasty, the number of Chinese confessing Buddhism as their faith has decreased steadily. Today, they are estimated to account for only about 6.2 per cent of the Chinese population (Laenderdaten.info, n.d.). Grube (1910, p. 156) ascribes the downward trend of Chinese Buddhism largely to the lack of binding dogmas, inadequate organizational solidarity, and the great gap between clerics and lay people. Nonetheless, Buddhism remains an integral part of Chinese society, including under the auspices of the Communists, and is thus further evidence of its adaptive capacity (Küng & Ching, 1988).

The Legend of the Buddha

It is not possible to reconstruct a precise biography on Prince Siddharta Gautama Sakyamuni, who later became known as Buddha, also known as the "Awakened One" or the "Enlightened One." Recent research, however, assumes that he lived in the time from 450 to 370 BC (von Brück, 2016, p. 66). Given this time frame, Buddha is believed to have been more or less a contemporary of Confucius (551–479 BC). His statements and speeches were initially preserved through oral traditions before subsequently being recorded in writing.

The fundamental principles of the teachings developed by Buddha are clearly apparent in his legend-driven life story (Cheetham, 1994). The story surrounding his birth reveals him to be a transcendent being, since Prince Siddharta is mythologized as entering the body of his mother, Queen Maya, in the shape of a white elephant. "Th[is] conception is an act in absolute spiritual purity, with no defilement of inherence or lustfulness, which, for Buddhism, is the root of all evil" (von Brück, 2016, p. 78). He grew up in the palace of his father, who was, at that time, regent of a principality in the border region between India and Nepal. Prince Siddharta lived a life of luxury and abundance. When the time was ripe, he entered into an arranged marriage as a young man, which produced a son.

Up to his 28th birthday, the prince enjoyed the life of a bird in a gilded cage at his father's royal court. In his years as a young man, when he left the palace for the first time he was immediately confronted with the misery of the world. He initially saw a crippled old man arduously making his way through the streets. During further excursions that followed, he spotted a decaying, sick man. At one point, he was confronted with the sight of a dead man being carried to his place of cremation. Deeply affected by the sight of infirmity and death, Siddharta returned to the palace. The suffering that he had registered caused him to cast doubt on the meaning of life.

During another outing, the prince came across a venerable, wandering monk who stated that he was in search of the truth of life. The prince was so impressed by this example that he decided to emulate the monk and continue his existence in monastic asceticism. He left his wife and child and embarked on his search for the truth and the meaning of life.

Legend has it that, as a middle-aged man, he entered contemplative meditation under a fig tree while on one of his wanderings. Through deep concentration and meditation, he discerned, as "first knowledge," the truth about human existence and the essence of the world: namely, life is always associated with suffering. As the "second knowledge," he became cognizant of the "natural law of ethical causality" (Schumann, 2004, p. 72). He was, at the same time, exposed to the teaching of Karma (Sanskrit for "action, work or deed"): good forms of reincarnated existence follow good deeds; bad forms of reincarnation follow bad deeds.

The Buddha became convinced that human suffering could only be overcome if humankind forwent the craving for life. During subsequent meditations, he also became aware of the multitude and form of his rebirths: from the very diverse types of animals and human beings to god-like rebirths. At the same time, the path to freeing oneself from the recurring cycle of life and death was also revealed to him, viz., entry into the nirvana as the "ultimate state of peace" (von Brück, 2016, p. 538).

Following this "enlightenment," and until he reached the age of 80, the Buddha continued to wander through the north of India as a teacher, gathered kindred spirits around him, established orders and captivated lay people. His death and, with his passing, his entry into the nirvana as a "great, complete extinction" (Schmidt-Glintzer, 2005, p. 23) is one of the central themes of Buddhist teachings.

Teachings of the Buddha

The life story of the erstwhile Prince Siddharta Gautama Sakyamuni and later the en-lightened Buddha Sakyamuni is reflected in the origins and key elements of Buddhist teachings. Its mainstay is the notion originating in Indian philosophy that life repeats itself in an eternal cycle ("the wheel of life") and that all living beings are constantly reborn. The aim of the teachings developed by Buddha is to liberate oneself from this perpetual cycle.

The imperative of the "Four Noble Truths" of suffering and its overcoming form an essential part of such self-liberation (von Brück, 2016, p. 117). Buddha says:
1) All life is suffering.
2) Suffering has its roots in human craving.
3) Recognizing this correlation is the prerequisite for entering the noble Eight-fold Path.
4) To ultimately overcome the craving.

Suffering signifies more than the mere torment and deprivation that comes with life but, above all, the "subjection to all that befalls oneself" (Essler & Mamat, 2006, p. 39). The way to ending suffering occurs through the "Eightfold Path" and its eight steps of recognition (Schmidt-Glintzer, 2005, p. 16 ff.):
1) Right view: recognition of the Four Noble Truths and understanding of the teach-ings of the No-Self (i.e., understanding of the fact that there is no permanent Self);
2) Right intention: renunciation of life; good will towards all living beings;
3) Right speech: avoid loquacity, defamation, and lies;
4) Right action: act in accordance with standards of decency;
5) Right livelihood: do not harm living beings when earning a living;
6) Right effort: pursue only positive thoughts. This includes trusting in the veracity of the Buddha's teachings (Schneider, 1997, p. 71). Trust researchers might refer to trust in the rules at this juncture.
7) Right mindfulness: mindfulness of the body, feelings, and thoughts;
8) Right concentration: focus on concentration and meditation.

Only the recognition of life as a path of suffering within the meaning of the Four Truths and a lifestyle within the meaning of the Eightfold Path can liberate people from the wheel of eternal rebirth and lead a person to nirvana.

Life, Death and Rebirth

The processes surrounding life, death and rebirth are depicted in Buddhism using a quasi-natural science approach that is founded on centuries-old traditional Indian thought. This notion is barely accessible in Western thought. This is presumably the reason why these topics are not even taken up by numerous scientific publications on Buddhism, and certainly not in the many popular science publications. Essler and Mamat also point out that the "processes which take place [in life] and in dying are anything but easy to expound" (Essler & Mamat, 2006, p. 73). This section aims to reproduce the Buddhist concepts of life, death and rebirth in a contemporary fashion. The statements made here, above all, draw on writings from Cheetham (1994), Essler & Mamat (2006) and von Brück (2016).

In the conceptual world of Buddhism, the human being consists of an infinite variety of elementary particles. The management of the mental and physical functions of the human being occurs through chemical reactions across electro-magnetic fields (Essler & Mamat, 2006). According to Buddhism, the smallest components of human life are in constant flux, undergo permanent change, connect with one another separately or as clusters, and then disperse. These elementary particles may range from being coarse in nature (the human body) to being fine in nature (energy). Against this backdrop, the notion of a human soul within the meaning of a permanent, identity-forming essence is alien to Buddhists (Schmidt-Glintzer, 2005). Similarly, the notion that, as part of the rebirth, something like a "soul" wanders from one person to the next equally has no part in Buddhist thought.

In Buddhist thought, the phenomenon of rebirth takes on a significant role: but what is it that leaves the body post-death and then enters another body or even nirvana? At this juncture, it is worthwhile addressing the predominant notion within Buddhist thought from the process of dying: According to the wisdom of Buddhism, the process of dying takes place in "eight stages of deterioration of the rough, to be precise: the decomposition from the rougher to the finer" (Essler & Mamat, 2006, p. 76). In the final stage of the dissolution process, the ethereal passes to the very ethereal and thus into energy. What is then transmitted to another body can be regarded as an energetic impulse: "It is thus not the coarse form of the manifestation of life but . . . the energy on a more subtle, reality level migrates into another existence following death" (von Brück, 2016, p. 178). This energetic impulse also includes information and/or impressions of past actions concerning the previous life (karma) that determine the fate of the new life. "The effect that these have in detail [however], this, to reiterate the point, remains the task of future researchers" (Essler & Mamat, 2006, p. 73).

Enlightenment and Nirvana

The phenomena of enlightenment and nirvana also appear difficult to reach at times. What Buddhism perceives "enlightenment" to be is revealed in the recourse to the fundamental recognition of the Buddhist belief that everything to do with life is suffering: suffering in the world; suffering from the world; suffering from the transient nature of the being and from the permanent rebirth of the human being. In the worldview of Buddhism, the craving for life, for lust and for change all underlie these forms of suffering. Buddhism postulates that the individual can only break away from the constraints of recurring suffering and rebirth if that individual "awakens" from their ignorance of these processes and becomes aware of the corresponding causal relations in terms of "enlightenment" – much the same way as the Buddha did during his meditations under the fig tree. This is the first step to liberating the individual from the entanglements of human existence.

Enlightenment forms the springboard for the way to salvation, which can extend across multiple human lives. At the end of this life comes the Fourth Noble Truth: the complete extinguishing of cravings and entry into the nirvana. This "way of recognition" includes the deeper penetration of the "Four Noble Truths," strict adherence to the "Eightfold Path" through increased concentration, profound meditation as well as an ascetic lifestyle in every shape and form. By managing awareness, the "three fires" (greed, hatred, delusion) will be extinguished and the person seeking salvation transported to a state of equilibrium and inner peace.

In this state, the already enlightened individual gains an increasingly more profound insight into the nature of the world and the forces that move it. The individual sees the "unsatisfactoriness" of existence with increasing clarity and discerns, with increasingly clear foresight, the ways and means that will lead to overcoming it. On the social level, the individual is filled with profound compassion for his fellow human beings. This is the basis for the Buddhist value catalogue, which attaches particular importance to the interpersonal values of non-violence, tolerance, fairness, and trust.

In the course of the processes of insight that have just been outlined, those seeking salvation gradually liberate themselves from every burden of the human existence and are ready to die. This is the final stage on the "path of purity" (Cheetham, 1994, p. 289). On dying, life is extinguished like the flame of a candle. According to the teachings of ancient Buddhism, as still widely found in Hinayana schools in Ceylon and South India in particular, the majority of those seeking salvation are excluded from nirvana. According to the Buddhist vision, nirvana is understood to be an "extinguishing of all factors surrounding individuality, a state of eternal calm; no activity whatsoever or connection to the world of suffering" (von Glasenapp, 1978, p. 185). Access to salvation befalls only those who subjugate themselves to strict monastic rules, in other words: only a monk. However, under the Mahayana school of thought, prevalent in China, a lay person who has led a virtuous way of life, while not being granted entry to nirvana upon their death, is allowed to enter paradise.

What did the Buddha say to his disciples prior to his death?

I am now redeemed for all eternity;
I have been born for the last time;
No new existence lies ahead.
Disciples: this truly is the supreme scared knowledge;

The knowledge that all suffering has dried up;
This truly is the supreme sacred peace: the abatement of greed, hate and delusion.
(Nyanatiloka, 2007, p. 103)

Buddhism in Modern-day China

Even though Buddhism has been on the decline since the Tang Dynasty, the impact of the teachings of Buddha continues to be felt in many aspects of Chinese culture to this very day: Chinese thought, the Chinese language and its literature, science and the arts have, in part, been influenced by the Buddhist body of thought.

Grube (1910, p. 158) draws attention to the concept of humanity entrenched within Confucianism. He argues that Confucianism had initially only understood this term to mean a mutualistic relationship – in keeping with the Confucian Golden Rule: "Do not do to others what you would not want done to you." According to Grube, the notion of humanity only grew to mean "human kindness" through the influence of Buddhism. Only by realizing that this value is anchored at the top of the Confucian value catalogue (Grube, 1910) does one become aware of the huge impact that Buddhism has had on Confucianism and, in this regard, continues to exert until today.

Buddhist influences can also be felt in Daoism, for example in breathing techniques, health and hygiene instructions, and also secret doctrines of alchemy. The predominant notions of afterlife in Daoism equally have their origins in Buddhism (Chen, 1964; Grube, 1910). These aspects of Buddhism have continued to affect contemporary Chinese life to this very day.

Buddhism has especially made itself felt in the arts field, however. Here, it is primarily the Buddhist sculptures that have largely impacted Chinese sculpting. In turn, the sculptures reveal Greek influences emanating from the Indo-Greek cultural links dating back to the era of Alexander the Great (356–323 BC). With their unmistakably Greek features, these monuments are therefore denoted as "Greco-Buddhist sculptures" (Grube, 1910, p. 160; see Figure 3.2).

The influence of Buddhism is also conspicuous in Chinese landscape painting, such as the paintings of the Song Dynasty (960–1279 AD), created by using delicate watercolour and brush techniques. In their effortlessness, transparency and fragility, the mountains, trees, rivers, lakes and waterfalls embody the notion of transience, in keeping with the characteristic features of Buddhist thought (Chen, 1964, p. 480).

Many of the cited Buddhist influences on Chinese thought are still perceptible in the present day: even today, the Buddha forms an integral part of Chinese life (Chen, 1964; Krause, 2018). This is not only true in everyday life. Modern-day scientific discussion is also enriched with Buddhist thought, including ethics-related questions that are not only of relevance in China but across the world as a whole. This impact is illustrated in the following observations by Brodbeck (2010, p. 46): "[It] should always be remembered that, in a world of mutual dependence, non-violence, tolerance, com-

Figure 3.2: Greco-Buddhist statue (Source: en.wikipedia.org/wiki/The Buddha#media/File:Gandhara Buddha (tnm)).

passion, fairness, and trust are the only moral actions that can be justified, which should increasingly replace the irrational habit of always wanting to strive for more."

In a worldview such as Buddhism, which, by its very origins, is aimed at the salvation expectations of monks, any search for directives in business dealings will prove fruitless. With its maxims of inner-worldly asceticism, deep-seated trust and love for one's fellow human beings as well as nature mindfulness, the value system peculiar to Buddhism is very difficult to reconcile with economic systems and their enshrined pursuit of dominance, profit and power.

Given this indifference to the world of business, it is hardly surprising that no leadership system is known to exist that is founded on Buddhist principles. Some time ago, one of the authors took part in a grid management training course (Blake & Mouton, 1992) for executives in Thailand. At the core of the grid management system are the dimensions people and task orientation. Thailand is a country with a strong Buddhist influence. A noticeable feature of this seminar was that the Thai participants leaned strongly towards the leadership form that is aligned to people orientation (and only minimally to task orientation). It is conceivable that these insights can be transferred to a Chinese scenario.

The treatment of the three world views that are central to China has revealed that, despite their very different approaches, they have mutually impacted one another and become intermixed in numerous ways. Even though far more than 2,000 years have passed since their emergence, a large proportion of the attitudes and behaviours of many Chinese continue to be influenced by Confucian, Daoist and Buddhist concepts and ideals. Confucian and Daoist themes have even extended into business life to varying degrees.

4 Conceptual Framework

For an investigation of interpersonal trust in intercultural joint ventures between Western European and Chinese companies, a conceptual framework has to be established that provides a structure for data collection and data analysis. In this framework, trust concepts from Western cultures as well as those from Chinese culture should be taken into account. The framework consists of three components (see Figure 4.1): (1) a cognitive component, (2) an affective-emotional component and (3) a component describing the contextual conditions.

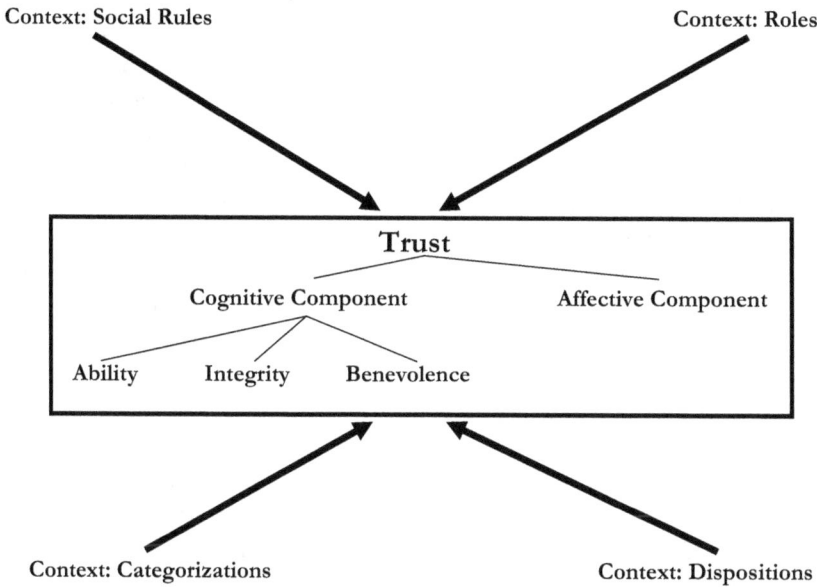

Context: Social Rules

Context: Roles

Trust

Cognitive Component

Affective Component

Ability   Integrity   Benevolence

Context: Categorizations

Context: Dispositions

Figure 4.1: Components and contextual determinants of interpersonal trust (derived from Mayer, Davis, & Schoorman, 1995; Kramer, 1999).

Cognitive Trust

At the cognitive level, interpersonal trust develops through the processing of information about a person with whom an interaction is intended, and that can influence the consequences of this interaction.[1] Mayer, Davis and Schoorman (1995) have proposed a model framework (see also Mayer & Davis, 1999; Schoorman, Mayer & Davis, 2007). They suggest that trust in a person is based on perceptions and assessments of the

---

1 See the definition of trust in Chapter 2.

https://doi.org/10.1515/9783111344560-004

trustor. Based on these perceptions and assessments, the trustor makes a prediction as to whether engaging in an interaction with that person (the trustee) will result in negative or positive consequences.

The perceptions and assessments of this other person can be categorized into three areas: ability, integrity and benevolence (see Figure 4.1):

- Ability: "Ability is that group of skills, competencies, and characteristics that enable a party to have influence within some specific domain" (Mayer et al., 1995, p. 717). Thus, the skills attributed to another person must be believed to enable that person to deliver a performance necessary to achieve a particular outcome.
- Integrity: Integrity encompasses several aspects. It is given, for example, when the trustee's behavior follows principles that the trustor considers acceptable. "Such issues as the consistency of the party's past actions, credible communications about the trustee from other parties, belief that the trustee has a strong sense of justice, and the extent to which the party's actions are congruent with his or her words all affect the degree to which the party is judged to have integrity" (Mayer et al., 1995, p. 719). The last aspect expresses the correspondence between what a person announces and what that person does. This can be understood as keeping one's promises.
- Benevolence: This aspect of cognitive trust expresses the expectation that the trustee has a positive attitude toward the trustor and that the trustor will benefit from this sympathetic quality of the trustee. According to Mayer et al. (1995), this also means that the trustee is not guided by the motive of achieving an outcome that maximizes his or her self-interest at the trustor's expense.

Since trust is characterized by the fact that the trustor is in a situation of vulnerability (Mayer et al., 1995), benevolence is of particular importance for interpersonal trust. The vulnerability of the trustor can ultimately only be abolished by the benevolent actions of the trustee. Therefore, it is reasonable to assume that in the course of a developing relationship of trust (at least in Western cultures), assessments of skills and integrity are of great importance in the early phases, while the benevolence accorded to the trustee is more important in later phases as their exchanges evolve (Mayer et al., 1995; Schoorman et al., 2007).

With regard to the influence of cultural orientations on interpersonal trust and its components, Schoorman et al. (2007, p. 351) assume that "culture can also affect the perception of ability, benevolence, and integrity and the importance given to each of these variables in the model." This study aims to contribute to the verification of this assumption.

Affective-emotional Trust

In the models presented for explaining interpersonal trust by Western scholars up until the turn of the millennium, only cognitive processes were considered. Only recently have theoretical concepts been proposed in which, in addition to cognitive components, the affective-emotional assessment of another person is formulated as a basis for interpersonal trust (e.g., Dowell, Morrison & Heffernan, 2015). In the publications presented by authors from Western cultural regions, the empirical findings on the relative importance of the cognitive and affective-emotional components in the development of interpersonal trust are not clear and therefore unsatisfactory.

In the present study, affective-emotional trust is understood as "subjective judgment based on moods and feelings about another person's character" (Dowell et al., 2015, p. 120). This trust component indicates the extent to which sympathy ("liking") is shown towards the interaction partner. It is postulated that this sympathy can facilitate the establishment and maintenance of economic interaction relationships to varying degrees.

Some studies have documented the importance of interpersonal relationships for business success in the People's Republic of China.[2] Building and maintaining mutual affective trust is of central importance in this context. After evaluating 43 semistructured interviews with Chinese businesspeople, Kriz and Keating (2010, p. 309) formulated a definition of trust from a Chinese perspective: "Trust (xinren) is the heart-and-mind confidence and belief that the other person will perform, in a positive manner, what is expected of him or her, regardless of whether that expectation is stated or implied. The parts of this definition that refer to 'heart-and-mind' and to 'the other person' reiterate that, while business may desire to form relationships with other business, trust essentially occurs only between people." Fang (1999) uses examples to describe how trust in China is reflected in politics, in the context of family and family relationships, in the country's regional diversity and as a component of entrepreneurial management styles. Frequently used Chinese translations for the term trust in an economic context are *xin* (信), *xinren* (信任) or *xin-yong* (信用).

With regard to business relationships in China, the *guanxi* concept is a central element of trust (Sievert, 2005), as Kriz and Keating (2010, p. 309) state: "The definition underpins the importance in Chinese markets of interpersonal over inter-firm relationships, which has been increasingly understood through the significant volume of prior research into guanxi." In addition, *guanxi* can become a sustainable, lasting basis of trust for economic relationships in China if it is supported by honesty, sincerity and personal sympathy ("liking"): "The combination of honesty, sincerity, and liking, together with positive cooperation, is believed to build *xinren*" (Kriz & Keating, 2010, p. 311).

---

2 Cf. the review of the literature in Kriz and Keating (2010).

Trust is thus not limited to the expectation that reciprocity will be maintained in business cooperation, as is typically part of the *guanxi* concept. Rather, trust often coincides with heartfelt feelings of sympathy and warmth, i.e., "liking." Thus, trusting relationships in Chinese culture often reach a depth that is seldom or never reached in Western cultures, because the relationship is one's only social capital. "To have trust (*xinren*) implies that you have a relationship (*guanxi*) whether the motives are intentional or unintentional; but *guanxi* does not have to include *xinren*. To have xinren . . . gives you more 'rights' with the person and will provide a stronger and more durable branch in your network" (Kriz & Keating, 2010, p. 311). These authors therefore also refer to Chinese culture as "deep trust culture." In particular, they cite perceived sympathy ("liking of words, tone, eyes, face, and expression") as an essential component of trust in Chinese culture. This aspect overlaps with the concept of intuitive trust according to Dowell et al. (2015).

Affective trust as a component of interpersonal trust has only rarely been considered in relevant studies by authors of Western origin and only a few years ago. The results of the study by Dowell et al. (2015) illustrate the importance of personal sympathy ("liking") in the development of trustful economic relationships in western cultural areas, e.g., Australia. However, empirical studies measuring the cognitive and the affective components of trust and discovering if the affective component adds incremental predictive power to the cognitive component in understanding how interpersonal trust develops are as yet missing.

Contextual Determinants of Interpersonal Trust

In addition to the cognitive and affective-emotional components, several contextual conditions are important for the development of interpersonal trust (Kramer, 1999, p. 575). These include (1) dispositional trust as a characteristic of the trustor, (2) the assignment of the people involved to social categories, which is undoubtedly influenced by the cultural orientations of the participants, (3) the roles that the individuals assume in the cooperation and (4) social-societal rules that influence the development and maintenance of the cooperative relationship between the individuals.

Dispositional Trust

Results from surveys and experimental laboratory studies show considerable variation in individual predispositions to trust others (e.g., Gurtman, 1992; Sorrentino et al., 1995; Payne & Clark, 2003). Theoretical considerations and empirical studies by authors from Western cultures have identified three determinants of this predisposition (Kramer, 1999): (1) expectations of an individual about the trustworthiness of *any* interaction person, i.e., generalized trust, (2) past direct experiences of the trustworthiness of particular interaction persons, i.e., target-specific trust, and (3) experiences of the trustworthiness of particular interaction persons as communicated by third parties, i.e., trustee reputational trustworthiness.

In international comparison studies, dispositional trust varies considerably, as Linggi (2011) shows using data from the World Values Survey 2000. Rather high dispositional trust is reported for the Scandinavian countries Norway, Sweden, Denmark and Finland, as well as for the Netherlands and the People's Republic of China. In a comparison covering 36 countries, the lowest values of dispositional trust are shown for the Eastern European countries of Poland, Latvia, Slovakia and Romania as well as for South Africa and Argentina. Influences on the development of dispositional trust can come from the form of government and the prevailing cultural orientation of the population: In countries with a long tradition of democracy, dispositional trust tends to be higher than in countries without a long tradition of democracy (Inglehart, 1998; Bornschier, 2005). Moreover, in individualistically oriented societies dispositional trust tends to be higher than in collectivistically oriented societies (Yamagishi, 2011).

Social Categorizing and Trust

Category-based trust refers to assumptions about the affiliation of an interaction partner to a social category. These often influence the assessment of trustworthiness without the trustor even noticing their influence. Brewer (1981, 1996) provides two arguments for the influence of social categorization processes on assessments of trustworthiness: (1) Perceived joint affiliation with a certain social category can serve as a rule of thumb for the trustworthiness of a trustee, and thus justifies why no information about potential risks of an interaction with the trustee is needed. (2) During the categorization processes, perceptions are often distorted in favor of in-group members: Trustors tend to ascribe positive characteristics such as honesty and willingness to potentially cooperating in-group members. In this way, assessments of trustworthiness arise solely on the basis of perceived membership in certain social categories (see also Williams, 2001). According to Yamagishi (2011), this is particularly true in collectivist-oriented societies. The considerations of Linggi (2011) confirm these observations (see also Jing & Bond, 2015).

Role-based Trust

According to Kramer (1999), role-based trust occurs when a trustor trusts (or distrusts) another person because this person assumes a specific role in the interaction with the trustor, e.g., the trustor may observe the trustee in a leader's role or in exercising a profession (engineer, lawyer). "Such trust develops from and is sustained by people's common knowledge regarding the barriers to entry into organizational roles, their assumptions of the training and socialization processes that role occupants undergo, and their perceptions of various accountability mechanisms intended to ensure role compliance" (Kramer, 1999, p. 578). The trust placed in an interaction target is thus based neither on an assessment of the person concerned along the cognitive and affective-emotional components nor on how well this person fulfills his or her role. Role-based trust reduces uncertainties about motives and abilities through processes of stereotyping: Whoever fills a certain role will very likely behave in a way that one (= the trustor) can expect from people who typically fill this role (Meyerson, Weick & Kramer 1996).

These expectations are shaped by the cultural orientations of those involved. An empirical study by Bueechl, Pudelko and Gillespie (2023) on employees of German–Chinese joint ventures shows that trust-building in the German–Chinese management context is fundamentally different from what has been described in previous management literature. Due to Confucian role expectations, Chinese employees tend to have a high level of trust in their German superiors right from the start. Since these role expectations are often not fulfilled by German superiors due to their cultural orientation and a lack of intercultural knowledge, this initially high level of trust erodes after a short time. According to Bueechl et al. (2023) the process of rebuilding trust that often follows depends little on the efforts and actions of German superiors.

Trust Based on Social Rules

The common knowledge of the members of a society about social, societal or legal rules that prescribe appropriate behavior means that these rules and their observance are not questioned (Kramer, 1999). "When reciprocal confidence in members' socialization into and continued adherence to a normative system is high, mutual trust can acquire a taken-for-granted quality" (Kramer, 1999, p. 579). According to Yamagishi (2011; Yamagishi & Yamagishi, 1994), rule-based trust is an explanation for the rather high values reported in surveys of dispositional trust for countries such as China or Japan. Among the members of these societies, there is unspoken agreement about the validity of the social rules. At the same time, the sets of rules in these societies have the effect that participation in economic and social life is hardly possible when trustees have violated the rules. As a consequence, it is not unusual for these societies to show preference for people belonging to the same group (e.g., people of the same nationality) and disadvantage for strangers who may not know or play by the same rules (e.g., foreigners) (Jing & Bond, 2015; Kramer, 1999).

The relationships postulated by Kramer (1999) form the theoretical basis of an empirical study by Muethel and Bond (2013). Based on data collected from more than 25,000 employees from 42 countries as part of the World Values Survey conducted in 2005–2008, these researchers examined determinants of trust in people of consistent and diverse group memberships. Their study is based on findings by Delhey, Newton and Welzel (2011) that individuals from more than 40 countries trusted in-group members (e.g., individuals of the same nationality) more than members of out-groups (e.g., foreigners). Muethel and Bond (2013) suspected the causes of this effect to lie in three aspects mentioned by Kramer (1999): dispositional trust, category-based trust and rule-based trust. Their data analyses show no systematic relationship between rule-based trust and overall trust shown toward out-group members. In contrast, clear connections could be found for the other two aspects: (1) If the development of high dispositional trust is successful in the course of the socialization of adolescents, then trust in out-group members tends to be higher. (2) In societies in which social categorization processes play a relatively minor role and in which a high level of equality of opportunities can be observed for members of all social groups, trust in out-group members tends to be high. Overall, the study by Muethel and Bond (2013) shows that the model framework proposed by Kramer (1999) is a sensible enhancement to the cognitive and affective-emotional models of interpersonal trust.

Problem Questions

In the present study, relationships of economic cooperation and in particular joint ventures between companies from Western Europe and the People's Republic of China are to be analyzed with regard to the mutual trust of the people involved at both top and middle management levels.

Specifically, answers should be given to the following research questions:

1. What experiences do managers of German–Chinese joint ventures report with regard to trust-building processes? Do managers generally express high levels of mutual trust? Or are there more or less obvious trust asymmetries? In what situations do German managers discern a high level of trust in their Chinese colleagues? When do Chinese managers discern a high level of trust in their German colleagues?[3]
2. Which components of the trust concept are of higher or lower importance for managers with different cultural orientations? Which of these trust dimensions or components are more or less important in trust-building processes when managers from China and Western Europe are involved?
3. What implications can be derived from the findings of this study for future cooperation between European and Chinese companies?

The present study will try to provide answers to these questions.

---

3 Similarly, Willinger, Keser, Lohmann and Usunier (2003), for example, examined similarities and differences in trust-building processes among German and French managers.

5 Method

The study documented here intends to examine the development of interpersonal trust in an intercultural context from the perspective of executives who are or have been employed in European–Chinese joint venture companies or have experiences of Chinese–European cooperation gathered in other forms of entrepreneurial cooperation.

The design of the study is exploratory in nature and follows a methodology that can be assigned to the research field of qualitative social research. In contrast to quantitative social research, when using a qualitative research method, respondents are asked to provide verbal information about their experience and their perceptions of reality, which is then analyzed in an interpretive manner. The aim of this approach is to have social phenomena and processes presented from the perspective of those involved and in their own words. In this way, insights are to be generated that relate to the individuals' cognitive and emotional-affective processes of perception, information processing and evaluation as well as to the social processes proceeding between them (e.g., Döring & Bortz, 2016; Lamnek & Krell, 2016).

Interpersonal trust can either be a prerequisite, an accompaniment or a consequence of social processes. It is thus part of the social reality of individuals. It is expressed in the coexistence of people or is brought about by this coexistence and by mutually related actions (Schäfers et al., 2003). Social realities are created through ongoing construction processes, which can be reconstructed in terms of their content and processes using approaches from qualitative social research (Flick, Kadoff & Steinke, 2015). The verbalization of communication and interaction events opens up possibilities for understanding these construction processes and thus makes it possible to identify the contexts of meaning that form the basis of the emergence of social realities. Analyses of written conversation recordings are intended to reveal associations of meaning (Flick et al., 2015).

For the present work, associations of meaning are of particular interest that may be perceived differently by members of different cultures in the course of their personal interactions and that each establish degrees of interpersonal trust. From the authors' point of view, the qualitative research procedure seems suitable for making such associations of meaning recognizable, since in this way the complexity of trust-establishing and trust-preserving processes can be depicted. The data collected by means of guided interviews are available in the form of written interview protocols, which are analyzed using the grounded theory method.

Grounded theory is a social science approach developed by Glaser and Strauss for the systematic collection and evaluation of qualitative data with the aim of generating theories (Strauss & Corbin, 1994). The interview transcripts refer to trust-based interaction actions in the intercultural context of international joint ventures between Chinese and European actors, in which interpersonal trust may be of relevance. The aim

https://doi.org/10.1515/9783111344560-005

is to identify starting points for a realistic theory of trust-based interaction in an intercultural context and to make them applicable to business practice. The pursued interest in gaining knowledge goes beyond the reconstruction of subjective views by trying to uncover the underlying culturally shaped social phenomena.

Of the 31 respondents, 6 were acquired through the Chinese branch of an international auditing and consulting firm. The remaining 25 people were persuaded to participate by a member of the author team in personal talks. A total of 15 executives were of Chinese nationality or origin while 16 executives were of Western nationality. When recruiting the respondents, a multi-stage process was followed according to the procedure of typical case sampling, whereby considerations of theoretical sampling were also taken into account. Typical case sampling is a variant of targeted sampling that can be useful when examining phenomena or processes in comparison to what is considered typical or average for members of a population. In theoretical sampling, it is decided on the basis of data collection that has already taken place and the experience gained as a result of which other (groups of) people should be taken into account when acquiring information. The executives surveyed are employed in the structural engineering and building materials sectors, in the chemical industry, in automobile construction, in aircraft construction, in mechanical engineering, in the service sector and in the agriculture business.

Table 5.1 provides an overview of the relevant characteristics of the respondents.

Based on the conceptual framework outlined in Chapter 4, a guide to conducting semi-structured interviews to collect qualitative data was developed. The interviews were conducted via telephone or Skype by a doctoral student from the Chinese University of Hong Kong. All 15 interviews with respondents of Chinese origin were conducted in Mandarin, the remaining 16 interviews in English. A total of 30 respondents gave their consent to a tape recording of the interview. One respondent refused this consent and, in this case, the interviewer drew up a memory protocol, partly during the interview and partly immediately afterwards. Before analyzing the data, the authors decided unanimously to exclude this interview from further analysis. The memory protocol could not reach the level of accuracy achieved with the transcriptions. This decision was unavoidable in order to rule out incorrect assessments of the recorded statements, which could have arisen due to the imprecise recording of what was said.

The 15 interviews conducted in Mandarin were transcribed by two native speakers and translated into English. The remaining 15 audiotaped interviews were transcribed by two members of the team of authors (Mayring, 2002; Kowal & O'Connell, 2003). In the process of transcription, the communicative information should be comprehensively preserved (Kruse 2006). Since the goal of many qualitative analyses is to reflect the complexity of human interaction, it is of great importance to describe events in the words of those involved and thus make the complexity of social processes comprehensible and transparent for third parties (Rubin & Rubin, 2012). For this purpose, the procedure of literal transcription was used. Text passages that the

Table 5.1: Characteristics of respondents.

Nr	m w	Age	Nationality	Employer location	Management position	Duration of employment with current employer	Cross-cultural experience
1	m	63	Irish	D	upper middle	2 years	> 30 years
2	m	49	German	D	top	10 years	< 10 years
3	m	48	German	D	upper middle	23 years	17 years
4	m	47	Dutch	D	top	14 years	8 years
5	m	48	Mexican	D	top	3 years	4 years
6	m	60	German	F	top	15 years	30 years
7	m	38	Chinese	D	middle	10 years	14 years
8	m	37	Chinese	D	middle	12 years	< 1 years
9	m	40	German (Chinese descent)	D	middle	3 years	has lived in D for 18 years
10	m	40	Chinese	D	middle	3 years	–
11	w	56	Chinese	D	top	13 years	12 years
12	m	57	German	D	top	> 3 years	15 years
13	m	37	Chinese	PRC	top	3 years	13 years
14	m	58	Chinese	PRC	top	13 years	14 years
15	m	46	Chinese	PRC	top	9 years	–
16	w	44	Chinese	PRC	middle	> 2 years	1 month
17	m	48	Chinese	PRC	middle	> 6 years	1 years
18	m	45	Chinese	PRC	top	> 10 years	11 years
19	m	49	Hungarian	D	top	16 years	> 11 years
20	m	40	German	PRC	top	> 6 years	24 years
21	m	56	Brazilian/ German	D	top	2 years	2 years
22	m	54	German	PRC	top	< 1 years	26 years
23	m	42	German	D	upper middle	3 years	7 years
24	m	58	German	D	top	35 years	7 years
25	m	45	Chinese	PRC	top	> 5 years	–
26	m	60	German	PRC	top	14 years	19 years
27	m	46	German	D	middle	17 years	4 years
28	m	61	German	D	top	9 years	1 years
29	m	47	Chinese	D	top	2 months	7 years
30	m	46	Chinese	D	top	10 years	2 years
31	m	63	German	D	top	35 years	–

two transcribers could not unequivocally convert into written form were presented to the interviewer, who was able to provide valuable information for understanding many of these interview passages. A few short passages remained unintelligible due to audio interference in the telephone or bad Skype connections. They could not be transcribed.

A structured coding procedure (Saldana, 2009) was followed in the subsequent analysis of the data. Here, open coding, axial coding, and selective coding were used to analyze data and develop the concepts and relationships between them (Strauss & Corbin, 1996). Research findings are presented as a series of interrelated concepts, and interview quotes are used to illustrate them (Locke, 2001).

Limits of the Generalizability of the Results

When interpreting and using the results presented, it should be noted that the research approach pursued here can be assigned to qualitative empirical social research. Qualitative studies serve to capture an empirical phenomenon in all its complexity and variety.

Quantitative empirical social research requires the respondents' willingness to provide information. Respondent samples should be of a certain minimum size and a composition determined from the point of view of representativeness. The goal originally formulated for the present study, to carry out a quantitative study, had to be discarded under the given social and political framework conditions (Stening & Zhang, 2007). Therefore, the decision was made to pursue a qualitative approach. Qualitative studies follow the grounded theory arguments made by Glaser and Strauss (Strauss & Corbin, 1994, 1996). According to this, an unbiased approach to the social phenomena to be examined must be ensured at the beginning of the acquisition of knowledge. Grounded Theory does not provide a set of rules for the evaluation of collected data that can be used similar to a recipe. Instead, special demands are placed on the theoretical sensitivity of empirical social researchers, their creativity and openness and their ability to form associations. These skills should help to find ways to come closer to the data in iterative processes and to recognize connections (Strauss & Corbin, 1996; Linggi, 2011). In the present study, data collection is based on questions that have been prepared in terms of order and wording, which served as the basis for the partially structured interviews.

The insights gained from qualitative studies can be incorporated into the formation of theories, including the generation of hypotheses; they thus become the starting point for further studies with which more representative statements can be made about the empirical phenomenon under investigation. Likewise, on the basis of the results of qualitative studies, recommendations for action can be formulated for concretely found relationship and trust constellations. However, qualitative data cannot claim any significance with regard to the representativeness of the results.

There are a number of effects to consider when assessing the results of empirical studies with regard to their validity (informativeness) and reliability. The present study is based on a survey of Chinese and European managers who previously volunteered to do so. The interviews were conducted using questions previously developed on the basis of theoretical considerations. It should be noted that the interview questions also capture the respective theoretical construct. Using content analysis methods, the answers were evaluated using various forms of coding and thus woven into a network with constructs related to them.

In the course of data collection, biases can occur in many respects. In interviews, respondents may tend to formulate their answers in such a way that they (1) reflect a positive self-image, (2) correspond to socially desirable behavior or (3) correspond to the interviewer's presumed ideas of behavior appropriate to the situation (acquiescence effect) (e.g., Bauer, 2009). To the knowledge of the authors, there are no empirical studies that allow a reliable estimate of the frequency and extent of these biases. During the transcription and analysis of the evaluated interviews, there were no indications that the answers of the respondents were subject to distorting influences.

Furthermore, there is a risk that stereotyping presuppositions or hypotheses of the coders might have influenced the results of the content-analytical evaluation. Thus, the coders' perceptions and assessments of the object of investigation might have gained inappropriate relevance and perhaps were verified at the same time. This danger was countered by strictly following the rules of coding and interpretation (Mayring, 2002).

6 Results

The previous explications on the status and development of empirical trust research show that the cognitive components of trust were the focus of considerations by authors from Western, i.e., European or North American cultures.[1] Kramer's (1999) considerations focus on the contextual conditions under which social relationships are established and influence the development of interpersonal trust. The affective component of trust only came into the focus of Western trust research a few years ago. After evaluating their data, Kriz and Keating (2010) concluded that the affective trust component is an important success factor in business relationships with Chinese managers.

The present study supplements and expands the knowledge about the structure and development of trust in intercultural economic relations between managers at top and middle management levels in European–Chinese joint ventures. In the interviews, relationships between executives at the same hierarchical level in German–Chinese joint ventures are predominantly considered. The results will show that the cultural orientations of the managers involved are an important factor in the emergence and development of mutual trust.

Overview of Statements Made by European and Chinese Managers on Intercultural Cooperation and Trust

According to the model framework described in Chapter 4, the statements made by the managers surveyed were assigned to content categories. In the following, statements that relate to the affective component of trust will first be considered. Then, the dimensions of the cognitive component of trust are analyzed. Later in this chapter, contextual factors are included in the analysis, which relate in particular to social categorizations, rules and norms of social relationships in joint ventures, and role expectations. Finally, statements on dispositional trust are analyzed.

In order to shed light on the general climate of trust in German–Chinese economic relations, the managers interviewed were asked to comment on the statement, "In China you must be alert because otherwise someone may take advantage of you."

One European manager complains that the behavior of Chinese people is difficult to understand and interpret correctly. In his opinion this has to do with the fact that people in Chinese culture tend not to show their true intentions openly:

> *I would generally agree with the statement that in China nowadays you must be alert because otherwise someone may take advantage of you. It is because you don't know if the intentions of all*

---

1 Cf. also the literature review by McEvily and Tortoriello (2011).

https://doi.org/10.1515/9783111344560-006

people you deal with are genuine. In China, people try not to show in public what their intentions are. (# 05/119)

On the one hand, this statement may indicate that this executive is assuming that his Chinese cooperation partners are "dealing in an underhanded manner." If there is any ambiguity about the intentions of Chinese people to act, this situation or position may give rise to a tendency to attribute unfair business practices to them. On the other hand, this statement may indicate that the manager feels uncertain about whether he is correctly interpreting the verbal and non-verbal codes in situations of intercultural communication.

One Chinese manager confirms that in many situations, because of the indirect communication that prevails in China, it is difficult or even impossible for non-Chinese people to find out what a Chinese person is thinking and intending:

> *I think Europeans are more trustworthy in most cases. Because they don't keep their thoughts hidden. They'd tell you if they have a problem with you, unlike the Chinese. The Chinese might not say anything to your face, even if they have something against you, for fear of losing face [面子, mianzi] or perhaps in order to save your face, or simply because they are of a lower status. It's impossible to know what they really think. A Chinese person might appear to be a very close friend of yours, but they would still keep a lot of thoughts secret from you. (# 14/655)*

One European manager makes a similar statement and openly accused the Chinese cooperation partners of wanting to take advantage of their European partners. Moreover, he claims that Chinese are even proud when cheating is successful.

> *In China nowadays you must be alert because otherwise someone may take advantage of you; this is what each Chinese sometimes calls wisdom. I call it the lie of cheating. So, I do not want to be tricked by the Chinese wisdom. (# 19/187)*

This statement reveals a prejudice against Chinese business practices. By pointing out that every Chinese considers a successful defrauding of his opponent as "wisdom," this respondent possibly makes a reference to the stratagems known from classical Chinese warfare, which consist of 36 instructions for a successful outcome (e.g., Verstappen, 1999; von Senger, 2000).

Chinese managers also see the risk of being cheated in business relations in their own country. One Chinese respondent justified his distrust of the Chinese with their socialization in a highly competitive environment:

> *It is true that in today's China, you need to stay alert in order not to be taken advantage of. Chinese people grow up in a highly competitive environment; they need to employ all kinds of measures to achieve their goals all the time, which includes using your relationship with your colleagues or their mistakes. (# 14/654)*

Another Chinese manager made a similar statement. Moreover, his statement shows that, in his opinion, the focus on rapid economic success leads to Chinese people acting in a very self-interested manner:

> *Chinese people are generally quite clever, but lack a long-term vision, in the sense that they are mostly concerned with things in front of them, and not things in the future. Chinese people have a strong desire to fight for resources. With so many people and so few resources, they are possibly more selfish than people elsewhere. (# 07/514)*

For yet another Chinese respondent, the fact that Chinese managers pursue their own interests is an explanation that there is a great risk of being cheated in China:

> *Of course, in the case of conflict of interest, some people might turn out not to be so good. We need to rely on our own judgment and spend more time with people we are friendly with, keep our distance from people if there is a conflict of interest or a feeling of estrangement. (# 17/718)*

One European manager stated that, before he came to China, he did not expect a clearly recognizable self-interested or egotistical behavior from Chinese colleagues:

> *It was a big surprise to me that my Chinese colleagues are very egoistic. What I observe is a high degree of egoism, in the company but also outside the company in the social environment of people. (# 03/076)*

This manager has observed that the Chinese also show their self-interest by exploiting ambiguities in the regulation of legally relevant issues to their advantage:

> *In China, I very often have the feeling that if there is a hole in the regulation then people read it and decide that it is up to them to interpret this to their own benefit and are then acting in an egoistic way. (# 03/078)*

> *Because in China people tend to interpret vague rules and regulations to their own benefit and then are acting in an egoistic way, foreigners might feel being cheated. (# 03/078)*

Overall, these statements show that both Chinese and European managers think that they need to be on guard to avoid being taken advantage of by Chinese business partners. It remains unclear in the quoted statements whether the above-mentioned self-interest orientation of many Chinese is being pursued for their own personal benefit or for the benefit of the collective to which they feel they belong.

These assessments set out some general conditions under which Chinese–German economic relations can be initiated and implemented. At the same time, they give reason to fear that the development of trust between German and Chinese business partners could be adversely affected under these conditions, especially from the perspective of European managers.

The Affective Component of Trust

The statements of the respondents on affective trust can be assigned to three areas: (1) the development and importance of close and friendly relationships, (2) the separation of work and private life, (3) differences in motivation between European and Chinese managers.

Development and Importance of Close and Friendly Relationships

The Perspective of European Managers

European managers report striking differences in their close relationships with colleagues. Close relationships between European colleagues in their own working environment are quite common. In contrast, the relations between Chinese and European colleagues are rarely described as close and friendly:

> In a company you have relationships which are somehow related to a task. You often have colleagues around where you feel a certain closeness and you may see a lot of similarities. With some of them, you may even go out privately together. Towards Chinese colleagues there is definitely a bigger gap. (# 03/072)

> I do not feel that working with my Chinese colleagues is like working with friends. For Europeans, working with friends means also singing, playing, and drinking together. This does not happen here. (# 04/094)

Two managers strongly avoid close and friendly relationships with Chinese colleagues. One respondent indicated that the reason for this was bad experiences in the past, which, however, were not described further in the course of the interview:

> I have learned not to feel that working with my Chinese colleagues is like working with friends. I personally have changed over the years. Today, I put this more distant than in the past, obviously because of negative experiences. (# 22/291)

> I get together in a social setting with my foreign colleagues in China, but I never mingle with my Chinese colleagues in a private setting. (# 02/044)

> I share opinions and ideas with them, and they share opinions and ideas with me. Feelings maybe is a different matter. I would not share feelings with my Chinese colleagues. (# 02/051)

One European manager even formulates a common cultural basis and the duration of cooperation as conditions for close and friendly relationships with people from the work environment:

> I do not feel that working with your Chinese colleagues is like working with friends. I think to really be considered friends one needs to have a longer history together and also to have a similar

cultural platform. I have a few Chinese colleagues that I would consider friends, but as close as my German friends probably not. (# 20/212)

In addition to cultural differences, a lack of language skills on both sides is given as an explanation for the lack of close and friendly relationships between Chinese and European managers. Few European managers have sufficient Chinese language skills. At the same time, some European executives complain that many Chinese managers show little or no motivation to acquire knowledge of English or even German or to improve their existing language skills. Overall, the language barrier has a negative impact on the formation of close and friendly relationships:

Working with my Chinese colleagues is not like working with friends. I think the distance between to be a colleague and to be friends is big here also because of the behaviour of the human beings after work. Sometimes the people are not getting closer, although they work together for two years. They are a little bit apart, because the interests are different. And the language is also a thing that separates people. (# 21/252)

Not all European managers share the view that close and friendly relations with Chinese colleagues should be avoided. Some of the European respondents report that the openness and interest of the Chinese colleagues make it easier to establish and maintain close and friendly relationships. They argue that it is important to get involved with the different perceptions and assessments and to look for "common ground":

Working with my Chinese colleagues is like working with friends, because they can be very open. The people who work closest with me are open, they always want to make activities besides the working time. (# 05/113)

The relationship with my Chinese colleagues I would describe as open; it's friendship. On the other hand, dealing with different views and perceptions and trying to build bridges between the different views and trying to find common ground. (# 23/338)

I feel that working with my Chinese colleagues is like working with friends. Of course, that depends on the personality, but it's really a good cooperation on average. The people are always friendly, always like to help, so that it's a very good relationship. (# 27/410)

The Perspective of Chinese Managers

Several statements by Chinese managers indicate that, from their perspective, close and friendly relationships with European colleagues are sought after and that Chinese managers tend to appreciate them. These close and friendly relationships are not only sought at work, but also in their free time, which some Chinese managers like to spend with their European colleagues. Here there is a striking difference to the perspectives of European managers:

We like making friends with them and do some activities with them together in our spare time. We want to have foreign friends we can brag about. We would like to become friends with our European colleagues. I am willing to be their friend. (# 17/711)

We are friends and working partners. In my spare time I am willing to become friends with them, but at work we each carry out our own duties and take our own responsibility. So, we have a serious work relationship and friendship. (# 17/715)

We have a work relationship, whether we are on the same level or different levels of the company hierarchy. But outside of work, I am willing to become their friend, have a good communication with them, and help them. We might also drink coffee together or go for a drink. I think we get along very well. As long as there is no conflict of interest, we are close working partners. (# 17/715)

We are each other's good teacher and helpful friend; we are also like brothers. We have a very harmonious relationship. That's the atmosphere created between my European colleagues and me. (# 25/755)

In three interviews, Chinese executives report on friendly relations with their European colleagues. However, these seem to be limited to the work area. One manager emphasizes that building relationships with Germans takes time, but that the relationships then are all the better. No statements are made about joint activities in the leisure domain:

I feel like I am working with friends when I am working with my European colleagues. Generally, they are very friendly, straightforward, and they are willing to make friends with Chinese. It might take a little longer to get to know and become close friends with Germans. But once you become friends, you will get along very well. We are friends with most of our German managers and we have a very pleasant time working together. (# 18/730)

I feel like working with friends when I am working with my European colleagues. The atmosphere is one that you have around your friends. The Europeans in general are quite simple. For them, work is work, and they don't get distracted easily by other factors. (# 09/559)

I feel like working with friends when I am working with my European colleagues. After spending some time together, we could tell whether a person is good or bad, and feel the warmth and humanity shown by each other. It's natural to have a relationship built after working together for a long time. Especially because we are working on the same thing, going in the same direction, we'd be like a family if we achieve our goals together. (# 13/622)

Separation of Work and Private Life

The Perspective of European Managers
Several statements indicate that European and Chinese managers differentiate clearly between work and private life. This difference can also be found in Trompenaars' culture model (Hampden-Turner & Trompenaars, 1993; Trompenaars & Hampden-Turner, 1997; cf. Chapter 2). Trompenaars differentiates between specific cultures (in which there is a clear separation between social relationships at work and in private and leisure life) and diffuse cultures (in which there is little or no clear separation between these areas of life). Many Western European national cultures can be assigned to the

specific cultures; many East Asian national cultures show characteristics of diffuse cultures.

A number of statements by European managers reveal that they want work and private life to be separated. However, some respondents also differentiate according to the national origin of colleagues with whom social relationships are maintained during leisure activities. There are leisure activities together with colleagues of European origin, but less so with Chinese colleagues:

> *I keep a little bit distance as a high-level leader. I don't want to come too close as friends. I think that is not good for my function. (# 12/141)*

> *In a company you have relationships which are somehow related to a task. You often have colleagues around where you feel a certain closeness and you may see a lot of similarities. With some of them, you may even go out privately together. Towards Chinese colleagues, there is definitely a bigger gap. (# 03/072)*

> *There are international and German colleagues in the organization with whom I occasionally go out privately. I never went out privately with a Chinese colleague. (# 03/073)*

> *I do not feel that working with my Chinese colleagues is like working with friends because for me friendship and working together are two different things. I am not so sure I would be able to work with close friends in my company. That's a completely different, a more personal relationship for me as a Western person than work. Work is a different dimension. (# 19/167)*

> *I have learned not to feel that working with my Chinese colleagues is like working with friends. I personally have changed over the years. Today I put this more distant than in the past, obviously because of negative experiences. (# 22/291)*

> *Colleagues and friends is in my management theory a difference. They are not friends, but you can work in a very friendly atmosphere. (# 28/445)*

Chinese colleagues are accused by some European executives of seeking close and friendly relationships with European managers for opportunistic reasons, for example because they want to derive personal benefits in the work sphere from developing social relationships:

> *It was a very big surprise to me that my Chinese colleagues are very egoistic. What I observe is a high degree of egoism, in the company but also outside the company in the social environment of people. (# 03/076)*

> *My Chinese colleagues work like a friend to me, but the reason is also because I will determine the salary package and salary increase. So, it's a question of hierarchy. Some of them work together with me as friends, that's true. But also here, I believe often that money is behind. (# 12/137)*

> *I would characterize a typical Chinese person as polite, straightforward, looking on their own benefit, their interests. (# 28/451)*

Their reluctance to make social contacts with Chinese colleagues is justified by several European managers by their belief that Chinese colleagues are simply not interested in close and friendly relationships with European colleagues beyond the work sphere:

I think it is not only a matter of me not being part of the group and not having a friendly or friend-ship-like relationship with my colleagues. I even observe this among my [Chinese] colleagues. They all go their separate way. (# 02/044)

I cannot say that I have made friends with my Chinese colleagues. This may sound harsh, but that's the reality. This does not mean that I don't work with them very well; on the contrary, I think I have to respect the separation between the private and the caucus sphere to be successful. If I were to mix this it wouldn't work. (# 02/045)

In a company you have relationships which are somehow related to a task. You often have col-leagues around where you feel a certain closeness and you may see a lot of similarities. With some of them, you may even go out privately together. Towards Chinese colleagues, there is definitely a bigger gap. (# 03/072)

Working with my Chinese colleagues is not like working with friends. I think the distance between to be a colleague and to be friends is big here also because of the behaviour of the human beings after work. Sometimes the people are not getting closer, although they work together for two years. They are a little bit apart, because the interests are different. And the language is also a thing that separates people. (# 21/252)

It's a big tension between the people; it's not open; it's a hiding a lot of things away from the other part; it's not fact-oriented; it's just what the boss said, even with the facts of physics. They say dif-ferent, but they don't care. (# 27/414)

The relationship with my colleagues from [our company's] team is target- oriented and really trust-worthy. But they still hide away once in a while, so still the one or the other is not communicating so openly. It's much better than before and much more international. (# 27/415)

We found a relationship which is very balanced. We learnt to talk very openly but knowing that – at least from our side – that there is – I don't like to say it – a hidden agenda. Of course, the man-agement has to take care also about political correctness. They have people in the background with their own interest and they have to convince many people in order to get the green light for a deep cooperation with a foreign company like ours. (# 31/481)

The Perspective of Chinese Managers

Several statements by Chinese managers reveal a different understanding of positive and friendly relationships with work colleagues. This understanding of friendship is reflected in the desire to maintain close relationships with colleagues, even in the pri-vate sphere:

Another example is the definition of privacy or the relationship between me and my colleagues or my clients. What's the difference between relationship in Europe and "relationship" [关系, guanxi] in China? Personally, I feel that Chinese relationship is purer and brings people much closer to each other. In China, if I say that I am in a good relationship with someone, we have opened up our private sphere to each other. If two Chinese girls are in a very close relationship, they are called (a woman's) best friend [闺蜜, guimi]. If two Chinese boys are in a close relationship, they are called brothers [兄弟, xiongdi]. They would share about their difficulties in family life, even conflicts with their children, parents, or spouse, talk openly about their own experience. But in Europe, people rarely talk about such personal matters. (# 07/509)

It's mainly the cultural differences. When we go to Germany, our colleagues are relatively quite friendly. After all, we are the guests from a distant place. As far as working, we get along with each other as colleagues. As we go to Germany first time, like guests from a distant place, we have some simple fetes off duty. It's not like in China, where colleagues are relatively warmer to each other, and they eat, drink, and sing together. The Europeans' career life is separate to their private life. So, it's not like working with friends. (# 08/531)

A slightly different attitude is evident in the following statement by a Chinese executive:

Also, you need to draw a line between work and life. Usually, you would unconsciously take your friendship into consideration when you're working with a friend. It's easier to focus on a matter without reflection on the person behind it when you're working with a colleague. (# 11/602)

One statement of a Chinese manager indicates that it is not always easy to establish and maintain friendly relationships with European colleagues. Some Chinese executives point out that people in China show great respect for foreigners. In contact with foreigners, this respect might make it difficult to build up and maintain relationships with colleagues in private and leisure life:

Most Chinese call the European or the foreign people "Laowai [老外]", and they would like to evaluate every foreigner kind-hearted, friendly and warmly, from the first sight. In China, we let them feel their priority as Laowai. Nowadays the situation is different because of the development of the country. Generally Chinese would like to treat foreigners very politely when they come. (# 08/537)

The following statement by a Chinese executive addresses three Chinese behaviors and motives that hinder the development and maintenance of social relationships between Chinese and European executives. First, the interviewed manager describes differences in the directness of communication, which are similar to Hall's differentiation between high-context and low-context communication. Second, it is found that the high-context communication that is widespread in Chinese culture means that people meet less openly: There is no open exchange of thoughts, beliefs and motives, which is why the Chinese must have the impression that they do not know one another well and that they are not really on good terms with one another. Third, the importance of *guanxi* networks is pointed out:

Europeans are frank, honest, and conscientious at work, etc. They are concerned with their own interest or realising their own values. The Chinese are more complicated. We are more concerned with building and maintaining our relationships [关系, guanxi] with other people, through which we could reach our goals or realise our own values. It's difficult to really know a person very well, so I never reveal myself completely to other people. It's much simpler with European colleagues, because they would let you know if there is a problem, what they are unhappy about, or what they think is wrong. They would point it out, so you know what they think. (# 14/653)

Five Chinese respondents express doubts that their German colleagues are interested in close and friendly relationships with their Chinese colleagues in the private sphere. Cultural differences are cited as one of the reasons for this reluctance:

We would not share our thoughts to German colleagues, which is not relevant to our work, because of the cultural differences. Certainly, they may not understand you totally, so this belongs to the life after work, has nothing to do with working. (# 08/537)

My European colleagues draw a clear line between life and work. They are very nice people and communicate with us in a fair way. But work is work. Our relationship is mainly based on work, which involves controlling and being controlled. But I have no doubt about their good qualities as human beings. (# 10/582)

Germans value their privacy very much. The Dutch are more outgoing and it's easier to become friends with them. Germans are more reserved. They focus on their job at work and tend not to talk about their feelings or private lives. (# 16/690)

Many of our European colleagues draw a very clear line between work and life. For our Chinese colleagues, that line is less distinct. They could still be working outside their work hours, making business phone calls, or negotiating. European colleagues are different, and they will also respect others by not contacting people on their holidays. Chinese people are not so concerned with this, especially if they're high up in the company hierarchy. This is a cultural difference I've noticed. (# 30/790)

The cultural difference between European and Chinese people is huge. Europeans have different values, faith, political ideas. I think they are more free and easy, inflexible. And they have a strong sense of superiority. (# 13/628)

Assumptions about Differences in Motivation between European and Chinese Managers

What motives do European managers perceive in their Chinese colleagues? And what motives do Chinese managers ascribe to their European colleagues?

Assumptions of European Managers about the Motivations of Chinese Managers

The content analysis of the interviews with European managers reveals that three motives in particular are ascribed to the Chinese managers: (1) a lack of openness in communicating with one another; (2) a clear self-interest orientation; and (3) following "hidden agendas" in dealing with European colleagues.

Several European managers complain about communication problems with their Chinese colleagues. According to the European respondents, Chinese executives are very reserved:

Chinese people don't necessarily show emotions very much. They don't necessarily show deep feelings. (# 01/018)

Chinese people are very ambitious, very hard-working, sometimes not as open as Westerners. (# 20/221)

I would not say so, because I understand "working with friends" is based on hundred percent trust. And for trust, I need to feel a certain appreciation and you need a clear authenticity between what people are saying and what people are thinking and this, according to my opinion, is missing sometimes. (# 31/476)

In relationships with their European colleagues, Chinese managers are also said to have a strong self-interest orientation:

It was a very big surprise to me that my Chinese colleagues are very egoistic. What I observe is a high degree of egoism, in the company but also outside the company in the social environment of people. (# 03/076)

I characterize my Chinese colleagues as young, willing to work, quite career-oriented, they want to be promoted, hard working. They want to go the next step to be a manager, to earn more money, to have a good reputation in their families. (# 27/416)

I would characterize a typical Chinese person as polite, straightforward, looking on their own benefit, their interests. (# 28/451)

In two interviews, European managers express concerns about entering into relationships with Chinese colleagues outside the work sphere. This is justified by political correctness and assumed "hidden agendas"[2] that their Chinese colleagues seem to follow:

It's a big tension between the people, it's not open, it's a hiding a lot of things away from the other part, it's not fact-oriented, it's just what the boss said, even with the facts of physics. They say different, but they don't care. (# 27/414)

The relationship with my colleagues from [our company's) team is target- oriented and really trustworthy. But, they still hide away once in a while, so still the one or the other is not communicating so openly. It's much better than before and much more international. (# 27/415)

We found a relationship which is very balanced. We learnt to talk very openly but knowing that – at least from our side – that there is – I don't like to say it – a hidden agenda. Of course, the management has to take care also about political correctness. They have people in the background with their own interest and they have to convince many people in order to get the green light for a deep cooperation with a foreign company like ours. (# 31/481)

---

2 In Collins Dictionary (2023) a "hidden agenda" is outlined in the following way: "If you say that someone has a hidden agenda, you are criticizing them because you think they are secretly trying to achieve or cause a particular thing, while they appear to be doing something else." In the context of the following interview passages, hidden agendas may possibly mean attempts by the Communist Party to exert influence.

Assumptions of Chinese Managers about the Motivations of European Managers

From the perspective of Chinese managers, the cultural differences and the associated attitudes and lifestyles explain why there is a generally low interest of European managers in friendly relationships with their Chinese colleagues:

> The cultural difference between European and Chinese people is huge. Europeans have different values, faith, political ideas. I think they are more free and easy, inflexible. And they have a strong sense of superiority. (# 13/628)

> Our European colleagues are from a different country, so they are different from us in cultural aspects and lifestyle. Therefore, it is not hard to understand why my European and Chinese colleagues each have their own groups, where people have a closer relationship with each other. We have different lifestyles, thoughts, work attitudes, and work styles. (# 17/717)

> Working with our European colleagues is not the same as working with my Chinese colleagues because of the language barrier, and also because of the culture, habits and backgrounds. We are different in all these aspects. Of course, language is a major part of the culture. (# 30/789)

Résumé

The differences regarding the affective component of interpersonal trust that could be found in the interviews can be summarized as follows (see Table 6.1).

On the affective level, the relationship between European and Chinese managers in international business relationships is largely limited to business-like relationships. Close and friendly relationships are rare. Since, according to the Chinese understanding, friendly relationships are an important prerequisite for the development of affective trust, the development of trusting relationships is inhibited or even prevented on the affective level. In the understanding of European managers, work and private life are areas of life that must be clearly separated. Friendly relationships, according to their beliefs, should have no place in the business world. European managers do recognize that their Chinese colleagues often have an interest in developing such relationships, but often it is suspected that the Chinese only want to use such relationships for their own benefit.

Many Chinese managers recognize that cultural differences, different lifestyles and views impede the development of friendly relationships with European colleagues. Communication problems also inhibit the development of friendly relationships.

Overall, a cool and distant relationship between European and Chinese managers can be observed in international business relationships on the level of affective trust.

Table 6.1: Similarities and differences in statements of European and Chinese managers on affective trust.

	Close and Friendly Relationships	Separation of Work and Private Life	Differences in Motivation
Statements of European Managers	– Relationships with Chinese colleagues are mostly not described as "friendly." – Many European managers avoid friendly relationships with Chinese colleagues. – Cultural differences and insufficient skills in foreign languages are frequently mentioned obstacles to friendly relationships with Chinese colleagues. – The openness of the Chinese colleagues contributes to relationship building.	– A separation of work and private life is desired by most European managers. – Chinese colleagues are imputed to seek friendly relationships with European managers in order to derive personal benefits from them. – Some European managers suppose that Chinese colleagues are not interested in friendly relationships with European colleagues beyond the working sphere.	– Chinese managers are seen as incommunicative when dealing with European colleagues. – In relationships with European colleagues, Chinese managers are said to have a strong self-interest orientation. – Concerns about political correctness and suspected "hidden agendas" are occasionally mentioned as obstacles to relationships in the private sphere.
Statements of Chinese Managers	– Many Chinese managers describe their relationships with European colleagues as work-related. – Many Chinese managers strive for friendly relationships with European colleagues, and some even take them for granted. – Cultural differences and insufficient skills in foreign languages are frequently mentioned obstacles to friendly relationships with European colleagues.	– Friendship means maintaining close relationships with colleagues in private life. – In China people show great respect to strangers. – Germans are assumed to be uninterested in friendly relationships with their Chinese colleagues in private life.	– Because of cultural differences and different attitudes and lifestyles European managers are expected to have little interest in friendly relationships with their Chinese colleagues.

The Cognitive Component of Trust

Benevolence

Statements of European Managers

European executives' assessments of the benevolence of their Chinese business partners are mixed. Some of the European managers interviewed indicate doubts about the benevolence of the Chinese colleagues in their current economic cooperations.

> *I would say that some of my Chinese colleagues would knowingly do something to hurt our company.* (# 19/169)

In relationships with European companies and their managers, Chinese colleagues are said to have a strong self-interest orientation. The self-interest orientation perceived by Chinese colleagues has already been addressed with regard to affective trust, because it also has consequences for the development of social relationships:

> *The central motivation of Chinese managers to enter a JV is to improve their wealth and their well-being.* (# 01/013)

> *The impression that my Chinese colleagues will do whatever they can to support your company is based on the ultimate goals of a JV. Benevolence or trust are not mentioned in this context.* (# 04/095)

> *I would say that my Chinese colleagues will knowingly do something to hurt the company, depending on their personal interests. Especially in the construction sector, there are always conflicts of interests, bribery or gifts by suppliers. So, I think, this is a very common occurrence in China. And, of course, it hurts the company. To a certain degree that's part of the local culture.* (# 20/213)

> *My Chinese colleagues work like a friend to me, but the reason is also because I will determine the salary package and salary increase. So, it's a question of hierarchy. Some of them work together with me as friends, that's true. But also, here I believe often that money is behind.* (# 12/137)

According to some European managers, their Chinese colleagues are also willing to exploit the weaknesses of foreign business partners for the benefit of Chinese companies:

> *I cannot rule out that my Chinese colleagues will knowingly do something to hurt the company.* (# 01/010)

> *I unfortunately cannot say that my Chinese colleagues will not knowingly do anything to hurt the company.* (# 03/073)

> *In China nowadays you must be alert because otherwise someone may take advantage of you, this is what each Chinese sometimes calls wisdom. I call it the lie of cheating. So, I do not want to be tricked by the Chinese wisdom.* (# 19/187)

However, some European managers perceive their Chinese colleagues to be benevolent, as the following statements reveal:

So far, I always had the impression that my Chinese colleagues have the right intentions. Maybe the way how they derive action out of these intentions for me sometimes is questionable. But, I never came to the conclusion that any of them would have a negative intention. And I think this is maybe also driven by the SOE[3] organization and mindset because finally this would mean you would harm the country. (# 23/335)

My Chinese colleagues will not knowingly do anything to hurt our company. Basically not. The company is considered as a second family in China. Sometimes when they will do something benefitting for themselves but not against the company. (# 12/138)

I am certain that there is nobody willingly harm the company. Why should they? No, they are here to make the company successful. And that's what everybody wants. (# 02/046)

I have the impression that my Chinese colleagues will do whatever they can to support our company, because if the company is not blossoming, they will hurt themselves. (# 26/384)

I feel that our team is very proud to work for [our company]. So, I do not think that our Chinese colleagues would knowingly do anything to hurt our company. (# 28/446)

Statements of Chinese Managers

In the interviews conducted with Chinese managers, both statements on the benevolence of European business partners and on the benevolence of most Chinese compatriots towards European business partners can be found.

In several interviews with Chinese managers, the European colleagues are ascribed a high level of benevolence:

I believe that my European colleagues would not do any harm on purpose to the company. I think it's the result of long-term education and tradition in Europe. They know their position and are loyal to their company. This is deeply rooted in their work values. There are clear-cut boundaries for them. It is one of their good qualities that they would not damage the company. (# 07/510)

It would not happen that our European colleagues would hurt our company on purpose. Because from the point of professional responsibility, everyone does the own job. From the point of scope of the group company, they all hope that every subsidiary in every country will develop very well. (# 08/532)

I do believe that my European colleagues would try their best to support our company. It's still a question of work ethics and morality. Germans would always try their best. (# 09/560)

I believe that our European colleagues do their best to support our company because they have a strong work ethic. It also has something to do with their frankness. (# 14/648)

I think our European colleagues wouldn't damage our company on purpose. I believe in their professionalism and work ethics. (# 16/690)

---

3 SOE = state-owned enterprise.

I feel that my German colleagues are very dedicated to their jobs, and they are working whole-heartedly to the benefit of our company, unlike us. We Chinese sometimes deal with private matters during work hours. Germans devote their working hours to their jobs. If they end up doing the company any harm, it's probably unintentional or a result of lack of ability, or maybe they made a mistake. But I don't think they are likely to do it intentionally. At least I don't see that happening to colleagues I work with. (# 17/711)

In one interview with a Chinese manager, on the other hand, strong doubts were expressed regarding the benevolence of European colleagues:

I cannot judge whether my European colleagues would do their best to support our company. All I know is that I would only cooperate with a foreign company if I have certain needs. That foreign company must also have its own needs if it decides to do business with me. (# 13/623)

The bosses of those companies usually have a strong desire to cooperate successfully with us, but whether the people they hire are also highly motivated to do so is a different matter. On the managerial level, I don't see it happening that they would try their best to provide us with what we need. (# 13/624)

One Chinese manager assesses the benevolence of his Chinese colleagues towards European business partners. Overall, his assessments are rather negative:

Our European colleagues see their own interest and the company's interest as the same. That's why I say they wouldn't do the company any harm intentionally. Chinese people don't always join a company voluntarily. They might end up in a company simply because they can't find anything better, so that company is just a stepping-stone. If they leave a good impression on the boss and are promoted, then the company's interest is also their interest and they wouldn't do the company any harm. But given the opportunity or power, quite a few Chinese people wouldn't hesitate to act in the name of the company for personal gain and even betray the company. (# 14/648)

When their own interest is not involved, most Chinese people could be trusted. But once their own interest is involved, they're likely to give priority to their own interest and forget about the company's interest. (# 14/654)

It is true that in today's China, you need to stay alert in order not to be taken advantage of. Chinese people grow up in a highly competitive environment, they need to employ all kinds of measures to achieve their goals all the time, which includes using your relationship with your colleagues or their mistakes. (# 14/654)

Integrity

Statements of European Managers

Three topics related to the integrity of Chinese colleagues are raised in the interviews with European managers. First, it is about business practices that European managers perceive from their Chinese colleagues and that they experience as dishonest and rather unfair. Second, some European managers complain that their Chinese colleagues tend not to stick to the promises made and contracts concluded with European business partners. Third, frequent misunderstandings in communication with Chinese colleagues are complained about.

The first topic concerns the business practices perceived by European managers from their Chinese counterparts. In the judgment of many European managers, Chinese managers are dishonest and not very fair when dealing with European business partners. This opinion is mentioned in seven interviews:

Culturally, honesty has a higher value in Europe than in China. (# 01/025)

Because Chinese people are more conditioned to being told what to do, they may not know what is right or wrong. (# 01/008)

Chinese people are the ultimate capitalists of the world, and they want to extract the best benefit that they can get. (# 01/012)

I cannot say that my Chinese colleagues try hard to be fair in dealings with other companies, especially with European companies. (# 01/012)

My Chinese colleagues are managing in a totally different way and that could put much more pressure on subordinates, pushing them into executions which a German subordinate would not consider fair. I think that's due to a different understanding of norms. (# 03/074)

Fairness and cleanliness in the business are important principles that appear in the European culture as an end of its own. I believe this is different in China where Chinese companies and Chinese bosses call unfairness and uncleanliness a wisdom. I simply call it the lie of cheating. (# 19/171)

My experience is that it is completely okay for a Chinese company to get advantage on others. They are so happy about when this happened even if it is an unfair advantage, because they believe that the leader was a genius, he has a lot of wisdom because he managed to trick another company even with illegal means. I am shocked that Chinese companies call themselves wise and very clever if they are unfairly getting an advantage of others. (# 19/171)

When Chinese companies steal your 'IP' (intellectual property) they use it for getting profitable and getting rich and they call it a wisdom instead of stealing. According to my values this is stealing because one company invested a lot of money to create something that has an intellectual value. The Chinese company is utilizing it for their own benefit and calling themselves wise that they are able to steal it and they are very happy about it. (# 19/172)

My Chinese colleagues are not very fair in dealings with other companies, especially with my European company. (# 21/253)

In the beginning of a contract the paragraphs are very clear, but in the end of the day when the Chinese see that my advantage is too big, then they change a little bit argumentation and say, "Yes, you can say like this but you can also say like this." Or: "I understand it a little bit different." (# 21/269)

Sometimes it's going beyond what I would define as fair, because it's not any more about facts but it's simply about trying to improve the benefit of your own company and then this is getting then too far for me. (# 23/336)

The Chinese colleagues from [our company's] team try hard to be fair in dealing with other compa-
nies, especially with European companies. The [other company's] team does not. [Their] employees
always talk about win-win, but in the end they have only one target, to get as much as possible and
don't care about others. That's very egoistic and not win–win oriented. They just say it, but they
don't do it. (# 27/411)

I think the Chinese government is not fair in dealing with European companies. The government is
not working towards business; they have their ideas to make China proud and independent. So, on
the one hand we feel being invited to go to China, but we now accept that we have to tolerate the
tendency in China that our technology is welcome, but it will never be protected from possible in-
fringement. (# 31/479)

The second topic of integrity addressed in the interviews concerns the reliability of
Chinese managers. Several European managers complain that their Chinese colleagues tend not to keep their promises and agreements with European business
partners:

Mostly the Chinese companies with international interactions learned how to respect contracts. I
generally have a better and better impression about contractual discipline in the business. But Chi-
nese companies never see the importance to really discuss several details, even on a daily basis
about a contract. I understand in the Chinese culture to rediscuss or saying that the contract was
done two years ago, so we need to do something else now. (# 19/193)

In China, it depends whether contracts are followed. Sometimes they promise things and deliver
other things. (# 21/268)

In the beginning of a contract the paragraphs are very clear, but in the end of the day when the Chinese
see that my advantage is too big, then they change a little bit argumentation and say, "Yes, you can say
like this but you can also say like this." Or: "I understand it a little bit different." (# 21/269)

You can have the nicest contracts, but people will simply not follow these contracts if they believe
they have a changed situation and they can benefit out of it. (# 23/342)

Or contracts. You sign even contracts and one week later they come to renegotiate the contract.
Why do they do that? They signed the contract. We negotiated two years, signed a contract now,
and one week later you want to cancel the contract. No strategic thinking, no long-term thinking,
just for them. (# 27/414)

My Chinese colleagues sometimes keep what they promise. When Chinese people say "I will do", it
means maybe I will do because he will never tell you in your face, in front of you they will not do.
Because they don't like to admit some weakness. They prefer to say more or less, and then not do.
But this is cultural, I think. (# 21/255)

In four interviews, doubts about the integrity of Chinese business partners are outlined as misunderstandings in communication with Chinese colleagues.

I know there are certain phrases and I know in China basically the words for saying no. I think it's
my responsibility as a foreigner working in China to have managerial capacity to be able to inter-
pret this. My response will be to understand what this really means and to get deeper, or to come

up with a compromise, but not to imply that if that person doesn't follow up, it means not keeping a word. (# 02/049)

I have the impression that what my Chinese colleagues say and what they do is often not consistent. I think this is a little bit the culture here. The people will not tell you directly the truth. They will rather try to make you happy first. (# 12/140)

My experience is that there is a tendency in China to show a bright picture to those who are coming from far away. My experience not only in my company but sharing it with other leaders is that Chinese colleagues have the tendency to show a bright, non-problematic situation especially to foreigners and make them believe that everything is on the right way and that there is no problem; there is nothing to worry. They are more trying to work on how the foreign boss gets a good feeling about the situation. In many cases, I unfortunately experienced that this is not true. If you look neatly in the background actually there are many things that are not going on. (# 19/163)

I do have the impression that what my Chinese colleagues say and how they act is sometimes not consistent. Many Chinese colleagues, and Chinese people generally, have a different and less direct way of saying things and expressing what they mean. And this can sometimes be difficult for Westerners to decipher. And on the other way round, many of us Westerners very directly communicate which can sometimes be difficult for the Chinese side to process. There must be many that will think we are rude or too direct or too open. (# 20/218)

Statements of Chinese Managers

The statements of Chinese managers about the integrity of their European colleagues are much more positive. In several interviews it is stated that European managers are considered fair towards Chinese business partners:

I think they would strive to stay fair when they are doing business with other companies, especially Chinese ones. We all know that fairness is essential for moving the company forward and motivating the staff. All the European friends I know are acutely aware of its importance. This is also part of their values. (# 07/511)

I think our European colleagues would try to be fair while doing business with other companies, especially our company. They execute our contracts well, which is fair because a contract is an agreement between both parties. (# 15/673)

Our European colleagues would try to be fair when they are doing business with other companies especially with our company. I think my European colleagues treat all their clients fairly. They have good work ethics. (# 16/691)

I believe that our European colleagues do intend to be fair. But sometimes they might not have a good grasp of what we consider to be fair due to cultural differences. (# 14/649)

I think in general they would try to be fair. But it's hard to say whether they are discriminating against the Chinese branch. It depends on the leader who has the final say, what he thinks of our company, and how much he's supporting us. If we are experiencing difficulties, would they do us a favour by not raising the price? There is room for manoeuvre. The problem is whether the leader is ready to support us. (# 11/603)

However, one Chinese executive expresses a different assessment in this regard:

I do not think that European managers would try to be fair to us. They are not down to earth enough. They are still applying their own ideology to our market. They might think their products are high-end, whereas in fact we have similar products in China already. They soon won't have a market if they don't change their way of thinking. (# 13/625)

In several responses from Chinese managers, European managers are credited with mostly keeping their commitments, promises and contracts:

I have no doubt that the European colleagues would keep promises at work. Basically, the German colleagues keep all their promises, unless they do not promise or they really can't realize it. They are not like Chinese, who can promise to say that they really do. German colleagues are more rigorous, in general they will never promise what they cannot realize. (# 08/534)

I never had doubts about whether my German colleagues would keep their promises. So far, all the promises they made, including those at tele-conferences, have been kept. (# 09/562)

Usually, our European colleagues will keep their promises. It is part of their culture that they either don't make any promises or they keep their promises, unless they really can't do it due to objective reasons. Many Chinese people make promises easily, but can't keep them, and they would make a lot of excuses trying to justify their failure. (# 14/650)

My European colleagues are mostly German. They are very different from the Chinese. They have more respect for contracts and agreements, and they have integrity. (# 18/726)

If our European colleagues make a promise, they will definitely keep it. This is part of our company culture. (# 25/754)

Europeans are better at keeping promises. They are more punctual. They stick to their plans. Their work plans are very detailed. European colleagues have had more training in documenting our meetings or discussions. They have advantages in co-ordinating compared to our Chinese colleagues. (# 30/793)

Four interview passages show that the European managers are attributed a rather high degree of reliability by their Chinese colleagues:

I think our European colleagues will do their best to support your company. My German colleagues are very reliable. If you give them a task, they will do their best to accomplish it. They will let you know if they have any problems. Their implementation or execution are very good. (# 18/731)

It's very hard to say whether they always do what they say they'd do, because it's impossible for me to know for sure. But on a scale of one to ten, I would trust them with a nine. (# 11/605)

I never feel that our European colleagues don't do what they say. Even if there are new developments during the process, they would let me know about the new developments in advance and inform me about the change of their plans. (# 16/691)

So far, I haven't felt that our European colleagues don't do what they say. (# 30/792)

However, two Chinese managers have formulated a much more negative evaluation of European managers' behavior:

> What they do is completely different from what they say. The boss might be really anxious to achieve something, but the staff not at all. They just do their job without worrying about the results. They are like young monks who chant the sutra and toll the bells everyday merely because that's a job they need to complete. They are not responsible for the boss' ultimate goal. So sometimes I feel that they are more like machines. As long as they do their job, they get paid. It's not their concern whether the boss makes any money in the end. (# 13/626)

> I sometimes feel that my European colleagues don't always do what they say. Sometimes they say they'll do something, but nothing happens in the next few months, and then it is simply forgotten. (# 10/584)

In a somewhat broader sense, statements on the motivation of European managers from the point of view of their Chinese colleagues can also be subsumed under the topic of integrity. In three interviews, Chinese executives emphasized the professionalism and positive work ethic of the European managers. One Chinese respondent addresses the thoroughness of task fulfillment and compliance with time targets by managers from different cultures. She finds that European managers are particularly thorough in fulfilling their tasks. For Chinese managers, on the other hand, meeting time targets is the priority:

> I think our European colleagues wouldn't damage our company on purpose. I believe in their professionalism and work ethics. (# 16/690)

> I feel that my German colleagues are very dedicated to their jobs, and they are working wholeheartedly to the benefit of our company, unlike us. We Chinese sometimes deal with private matters during work hours. Germans devote their working hours to their jobs. If they end up doing the company any harm, it's probably unintentional or a result of lack of ability, or maybe they made a mistake. But I don't think they are likely to do it intentionally. At least I don't see that happening to colleagues I work with. (# 17/711)

> If you assign the same piece of work to a German and a Chinese person, the German will make sure the quality is good enough, whereas the Chinese person will make sure it's finished before the deadline. So, Germans put quality first, whereas Chinese people put time first. Germans want to solve the problem to their satisfaction, regardless of the deadline. If it takes too long, they will ask to postpone the deadline. The Chinese will try to finish the job as well as they can before the deadline. (# 18/727)

One Chinese executive complains that European managers are less motivated to work hard, and instead tend to be lazy:

> A Chinese person would think about how much value or money they are going to make for their boss this year. We ask our staff to take responsibility for their own actions, to set a goal, and they are evaluated at the end of the year. Foreigners are so different. Foreign employees lack a sense of responsibility. They just do the things on the list, and not care about the results. (# 13/627)

> The work ethic of my European colleagues is alright, except that they are a bit lazy and inflexible. (# 13/623)

In summary, the statements made by European and Chinese executives show the following assessments:

(1) In the judgment of their Chinese colleagues, European managers are reliable and fair. They (mostly) keep to promises and contracts.

(2) European managers are seen as unmotivated and inflexible by their Chinese colleagues; one Chinese executive even describes them as lazy.

(3) From the point of view of European managers, Chinese colleagues are seen as dishonest and unfair when dealing with foreign business partners.

(4) In the opinion of the European managers, Chinese managers tend not to stick to promises and contracts. They tend to embellish the business situation in cooperations and thus do not describe the actual circumstances.

(5) European managers complain about frequent misunderstandings when communicating with their Chinese colleagues.

Abilities/Skills

The statements made by European executives about the skills perceived by their Chinese colleagues relate to three topics: knowledge of facts and methods, knowledge of foreign languages and the ability to make decisions and get things done. Chinese executives also mentioned three topics regarding their European colleagues: knowledge of facts and methods, knowledge of the Chinese market and the speed of decision-making.

Statements of European Managers

Two European managers mention the very good knowledge of facts and figures as well as the good method skills of their Chinese colleagues:

> The technical skills of my Chinese colleagues are excellent. And they are very detail-oriented. I admire their memories; they know every kind of fact and figures. I could call them in the middle of the night and ask them for some market figure in some region of China, and they would know the answer immediately. (# 02/040)

> My Chinese colleagues' memories and breadth of facts has to do with the education system in China. That's simply by the virtue of the fact that you have to memorize so many characters. And the Chinese workers are simply used to memorizing and reproducing facts at any time. (# 02/041)

> I think my Chinese colleagues are successful in what they do. Many of them have a very good education basis based on the education system. People are generally used to do what they have learnt or what they got from the teacher or from their supervisor and implement it. And maybe they are also very good in memorizing certain ways of doing things, so they are good in repeating and following. (# 23/332)

One European manager in particular emphasized the intuition of Chinese managers for successful cooperation with government departments in China.

> The people know very well what they want and where to go. They know their markets quite well. They know their customers quite well and they have a good sense of how to collaborate with the government and how to adapt to the latest requirements and implement good measures that follow the instructions that we have. (# 23/330)

Communication problems are frequently mentioned by the European managers. The reason given for this is the reluctance of Chinese colleagues, especially from rural areas in China, to learn languages and the resulting lack of foreign language skills.

> 95% of my colleagues cannot speak English. They are local people and the communication is one of the issues that brings sometimes a little bit misunderstanding or problems in the communication. (# 21/244)

> When it comes to the requirements of an international and global company, then you have to look more eagerly. You do not have that many choices, and it's a matter of language. You have different codes of understanding, especially when it comes to quality. (# 22/248)

> This somehow gives credit to people that speak better English. This is the one bias that you always have to live with despite of using a translation, but certainly there is a small bias that you have in an aspect. (# 23/328)

European managers perceive deficits in their Chinese colleagues in terms of their suitability for taking on managerial responsibility (cf., e.g., also Bass, 1981). The Chinese colleagues are attested to have little willingness and ability to make decisions as well as a lack of assertiveness. Some of the European managers state that this applies in particular to Chinese executives from state-owned companies:

> My Chinese colleagues lack a little bit synthesizing and interpreting findings, interpret them and derive conclusions and working a vision. (# 02/041)

> The Chinese colleagues have problems when it comes to designing and developing new processes, new tools. (# 03/071)

> Chinese people do not want to act on their own. They always want to get align and want to get instructions from the boss. Some of them are very hard to convince that they have a certain freedom to operate in their activities. (# 19/165)

> However, in many cases objective setting is not enough. In China I realized many times that to reach the objective, many Chinese people need basically a clear manual as well how to do it. So, they might follow something what the boss said because they try to avoid any potential mistake that they could do. Although they are reaching their objectives very fast when there is a clear pathway leading to the objective. But, when you lead them only to the objectives, that might be sometimes hard. (# 19/166)

> When you face new situations where there is no playbook yet written how to approach this, this is where many Chinese are struggling to find a solution. On average they are facing more difficulties

if they come to a completely new situation and then have to find solution quickly that would fit to that moment. (# 23/333)

A state-owned enterprise person is trained for thirty years to make no decision at all. So, this is a very very different approach, because in state-owned enterprise, if you take decisions you take responsibility. And if you take responsibility and you take the wrong decision you are not valuable to be promoted anymore. So that's the reason why they don't take any decisions. (# 27/407)

They are not trained to think out of the box. They are trained to do what they are told. And many of them don't look left and right, just do what they are told. That's really related to the school system. (# 27/409)

Statements of Chinese Managers

In many interviews with Chinese managers, the good knowledge of facts and methods of the European colleagues is emphasized:

I have a lot of faith in the quality of their higher education. They tend to teach you skills instead of single knowledge points. Those skills would enable you to find solutions to problems you might encounter at work in the future, and that problem solving process is also a learning process. (# 09/558)

I would share my opinions, feelings, or problems openly with my European colleagues. Their judgments are usually based on logic and science, so the more open I am, the more information I provide them with, the more accurate their feedback will be. (# 07/513)

Being occupied in a position, their professional skills, professional backgrounds, including the time they are on this position, is very long. Furthermore, the training system for staff in Germany is relatively speaking quite complete. And they know very well about legal regulations, including on the technical level. So, to say, they have professional people doing professional works. (# 08/529)

The technicians are conscientious, almost perfectionistic. They try their best to do their job well, which is a very good thing. They actually hold themselves to the same standards they are used to in Europe when they are doing a project in China, so the project quality is very good. Our Chinese teams cannot reach the same standard. (# 15/671)

Europeans are better at keeping promises. They are more punctual. They stick to their plans. Their work plans are very detailed. European colleagues have had more training in documenting our meetings or discussions. They have advantages in co-ordinating compared to our Chinese colleagues. (# 30/793)

In one interview, however, doubts about some of the leadership and managerial qualities of European managers are stressed.

I have no question about the professional skills European workers have, but you need to make detailed arrangements and be clear about what they should do, otherwise they won't be able to do the job well. You can't expect them to act on their own initiative. (# 13/619)

Some Chinese managers perceive deficits in the market knowledge of their European colleagues. In particular, the legal and socio-cultural framework of business activities are mentioned here.

> *I would not really be willing to let our European colleagues be in complete control of the future of our company. They don't really know the Chinese market that well, and it's not really feasible to control our company in China from so far away. (# 11/600)*

> *If I were the boss, I wouldn't let Europeans control my company's future, because they don't understand Chinese culture, business environment or laws as well as we do. If the boss of our company were me or another Chinese person, we would be responsible for the future of our company and wouldn't give our European colleagues all the power. (# 14/645)*

> *A Chinese person would be more familiar with the business environment, legal system in China, and people's mind-sets, which is a big advantage for them to do the job well. (# 14/659)*

> *Some of my foreign colleagues say that the most difficult thing for doing business in China is to cope with the change of policies. That's why I think it's better to leave jobs related to sales, marketing, and government policies to our Chinese colleagues. (# 29/771)*

Two Chinese managers address the fact that their European colleagues need a lot of time to prepare decisions. Since the Chinese markets are characterized by a particularly high level of dynamism, this deficit is of considerable importance for some of the Chinese managers:

> *Europeans divide the work into too many parts. The consequence is that for the same problem that one department could solve in China, you might need to communicate with three departments in Europe, with more detailed information as feedback of course. They would analyse all the risks that might be involved. But, that slows down the procedure. (# 07/503)*

> *European managers are reliable partners, but generally lack the spirit of adventure, and they are a bit slow in accepting new things. They work in an organised way and always plan ahead but are relatively slow in reacting to revolutions or crisis. (# 07/512)*

> *I would not like to let my European colleagues totally control the future of our company. German and Chinese firms are different because of the different national conditions. Due to cultural differences and different cognition levels, they know China the way as we know foreign countries. In China, the national conditions and the market are changing very quickly. But in Germany, even in Europe, the markets will not change over many years. The speed of development of China is very quick, and so the market and business chances in China. (# 08/528)*

> *In terms of the cultural difference between China and Germany, it can also be understood why the Chinese colleagues always take the first minute to grab the market. If we really research and develop a product like Germany or other European countries, taking a half to one year, perhaps you have lost the chance. (# 08/531)*

Table 6.2: Similarities and differences in statements of European and Chinese managers on cognitive trust.

	Ability	Benevolence	Integrity
Statements of European Managers	– The Chinese colleagues are said to have very good factual as well as methodological knowledge. – A lack of foreign language skills and a low willingness to learn languages are observed among Chinese colleagues. – Chinese colleagues are supposed to show low levels of decision-making willingness and ability and a low degree of assertiveness.	– Chinese colleagues are generally viewed as having a low level of benevolence. – In relationships with European companies, Chinese colleagues are said to have a strong self-interest orientation. – Chinese managers are imputed to exploit weaknesses of foreign business partners for the benefit of Chinese companies. – Chinese managers are supposed to be benevolent only in relationships with Chinese companies.	– Chinese managers are considered dishonest and not fair in their dealings with European business partners. – Chinese colleagues tend not to stick to promises made and contracts concluded with European business partners. – Frequent misunderstandings in communication with Chinese colleagues are complained about.
Statements of Chinese Managers	– The European colleagues are said to have good knowledge of facts and methods. – A lack of market knowledge is observed among our European colleagues. – The slowness and tentativeness of European colleagues in preparing decisions is observed.	– European managers are credited with a high level of benevolence.	– European colleagues are considered fair towards Chinese business partners. – European colleagues usually stick to their commitments, promises and contracts. – European colleagues are mostly considered reliable. – European colleagues are less motivated to work hard. They tend to be lazy.

Résumé

Regarding cognitive trust, the relationship between German and Chinese managers in international business relationships is characterized by asymmetrical distrust. European managers clearly question the benevolence and integrity of their Chinese colleagues. Moreover, they complain that Chinese managers do not make sufficient use of their acknowledged good methodological and detailed knowledge when decisions have to be made. Chinese managers tend to place a high level of trust in their European colleagues in terms of benevolence and integrity and credit them with good technical and methodological knowledge but complain of insufficient motivation for "hard work" and dynamism in decision-making. Insufficient knowledge of the market is also complained about. European managers employed by a Chinese company for longer periods apparently do not distrust their Chinese colleagues. The results are summarized in Table 6.2.

Overall, the relationship between European and Chinese managers is burdened mainly by asymmetries on the level of cognitive trust. The extent of this burden is determined by case-specific context factors.

Context Factors

In the model framework suggested for this study (see Chapter 4), four factors were taken into account that can influence trust-building processes in economic cooperation as contextual conditions (Kramer, 1999). Two of these factors, social categorization and dispositional trust, describe cognitive state or process variables that fundamentally influence the behavior of those involved. The remaining two factors relate to the rule systems characterized by law and the social norms that apply in Chinese society, as well as to the roles in which those involved in economic cooperation come into contact.

Social Categorization and Trust

Relationships between social categorizations and trust are addressed in the interviews with reference to four topics:
- *guanxi*
- reciprocity
- staffing in companies
- use of information sources in a fictitious used car purchase scenario

Guanxi

Statements of European Managers

Many statements by European managers indicate that the Chinese social concept of *guanxi*[4] is widely known among European managers:

> The parental relationship is extremely important. They are supporting each other in their own guanxi. In their guanxi they are really supporting. But outside their guanxi they are not very helpful to each other. Maybe they are more ignorant to people who don't belong to their guanxi. (# 19/180)

> They are good to those who are belonging to the core guanxi and in many other cases I also realized that they just don't care about what's happening outside in certain respect. (# 19/181)

> Whenever Chinese persons are together in their community, in their family then there is a strong connection, a very strong relationship, but for everybody not being part of that community I am not sure whether they take care of each other then very much. (# 24/369)

Statements of Chinese Managers

For many Chinese respondents, mutual support in close social relationships is part of Chinese culture. The social norm of *guanxi* is explicitly addressed in three interviews:

> In China you are more likely to get help from people you have a long-term relationship with when you need it because the trust is there. We believe that people you've helped would return your favour one day when they can. (# 07/519)

> In China it's important to build up a guanxi relationship. Our society is based on this kind of relationship. Europeans hardly pay any attention to it. (# 15/671)

> I think people I've known for a long time would definitely help me when I have difficulty. I think a friendship or favour should be reciprocal. I help the others, and I believe it deepens our relationship, and they will also help me in return. Of course, I will consider whether what I am asking from my friend is in their power. I won't ask them to do something beyond their power. It's part of the Chinese culture. (# 16/699)

Reciprocity

Statements of European Managers

Guanxi and reciprocity are closely related norms of Chinese culture. Nevertheless, they are addressed separately in the interviews and are therefore treated here as different topics.

---

4 Cf. Chapter 4.

Some European managers emphasize that in Chinese culture there is a positive correlation between the duration and quality of a social relationship and the obligation to provide social support – the longer a relationship has existed in China and has proven itself, the closer the obligation to provide mutual support:

An incredibly important part of Chinese culture is that the longer your relationship, the deeper your relationship, the more you have experienced together, the more likely that person is to be there and to help you in cases where you're actually in need. I think this is in a certain way the same as in Germany, but I think it's even more prevalent in China. (# 20/231)

I would consider it as true that in China, a person with whom you have had a long relationship is likely to help you when you need it. If you know a person for a longer time, they have examples why he can trust you and why he can help you once or twice or three times. And he also can imagine, OK, when the situation is played in the opposite, if I need your help, you also will help me. So, I can trust you now because the next time you will also help me. (# 21/272)

In China a person with whom you have had a long relationship is likely to help you when you need help. I experienced it a hundred times. So, whenever we have a good relationship with some suppliers and we came into a trouble, they immediately helped us. (# 27/427)

Statements of Chinese Managers

The rule of reciprocity is also addressed in some statements of Chinese managers. Obligations for mutual support are also addressed, but framework conditions are formulated for when these obligations are to be fulfilled.

In three interviews, the rule of reciprocity is specified to the extent that support in China is to be granted in emergency situations, but not in poverty:

When you really have problems, there is a common saying: we help people in urgency but not in poverty. If you are in urgency your friends will come to help you. If you are always in a poor situation, you are idle, mostly people would not help you. (# 08/546)

In China, a friend is someone who would help you when you're facing difficulties in life. That's what we call a friend. (# 10/590)

In China, people you have a long-term relationship with are very likely to help you when you have difficulty. If we have a long-term friendship and stay in contact, then they will help me when I need it. (# 30/798)

In one interview, the obligation of reciprocity towards strangers is specified – strangers must have acquired a positive reputation before they can assume that they can rely on the reciprocity rule:

Before working with a stranger, we would also make an assessment basing on the comments of his friends, business partners, or people who know him. If people say, "no comment", then usually there is something wrong with them. But if the feedback is generally positive, then we know this person could be trusted. (# 15/679)

Staffing in Companies

The interviews explicitly asked about the procedure for staffing vacancies in companies. This was done so because of indications that membership in certain social categories (family members, friends and acquaintances) is more important as a selection criterion for staffing in Chinese companies than other selection criteria, e.g., individual skills (e.g., Bond, 1986, 1991). With the question of the procedure for staffing, the present study intends to examine whether this procedure is still in use in international joint ventures in China today.

Statements of European Managers

European managers working in international joint ventures consider giving preference to family members of those already employed in the company to be unthinkable and fundamentally reject such an approach. Reference is occasionally made to compliance rules that apply to the (German) parent company and that have also been adopted for the international joint venture:

> When I need new staff, I would hire someone with the right profile, regardless of his background. Somebody being a family member of a Chinese colleague would not make it an easier choice. For me that would be an objection. (# 04/104)

> The European way of thinking is that when family members are coming together in a company, they are covering each other if something goes wrong. They hardly can be objective when we are tackling the problem. (# 19/198)

> I would not favour a family member of one of our employees. Because the family ties are in that case closer than the ties to the company. We don't want to build up a gang within our own company. (# 20/233)

> When in my company there is an important position that I need to staff with a new person, I will prefer not to hire a family member of an employee. I prefer not to mix the thing. I don't think that family in groups inside of companies are positive in some things. Sometimes if you have a great number of family members inside the company, sometimes you have fight between these family members. And sometimes they think that more complex only because of the situation that the other person is a family member. You cannot treat the person free. You've always to say, ah, OK, but this is the mother or the brother-in-law or . . . and so on. It makes the things more complex. (# 21/273)

> We try to avoid to hire family members of employees. Our compliance rules in Germany prohibit this. (# 31/491)

Statements of Chinese Managers

For several Chinese managers, giving preference to family members of those already employed in the company is also unthinkable in procedures for filling staff positions:

I don't usually take the family members into consideration when an important position in the company needs to be staffed. Different departments of a company have their corresponding responsibility, with confidential information involved sometimes. We don't want to see those information being shared among family members. (# 07/519)

In principle, the family or blood relations is not allowed for important positions. This is also not allowed in most Chinese companies. (# 08/546)

If we hire family members of present employees, then I would worry that they might form a sort of clique. (# 09/571)

Hiring a family member of a present employee might cause problems for future work. Chinese people value their relationships, and they don't always make a decision basing on the rules. If you are working with a family member, then you need to take more into consideration, and it would affect your judgments and decisions. (# 10/590)

I don't like the idea of couples or brothers working in our company side by side. Personally, I think it's a bad idea because family members or friends are likely to form small groups in the company which could have a bad impact on the management of the company as a whole. (# 14/659)

I don't really like family members working for the same company. With too much feelings or emotions involved, people would not put work first anymore, or they might not treat problems objectively. (# 16/700)

We try to avoid hiring family members of a current employee. Even if it's unavoidable, we will try not to let them work in the same department. (# 29/780)

In three interviews, however, preference for members of certain social categories is mentioned as a possibility:

If the applicants are both qualified for the job, then I'd choose the family member of a current employee. (# 13/635)

If a very important post in your company becomes vacant, I would give a preference to family members of a current employee, but only if they meet our requirements. They would learn about the culture of our company quicker from their family members. (# 15/681)

When an important position in our company needs to be staffed, we may give a chance to family members of a current employee. It depends on the circumstances. They have to be suited to the job. (# 25/762)

Use of Information Sources in a Fictitious Used Car Purchase Scenario

Social categorization also seems to play a role when information is needed in risky situations. In China, belonging to a particular social category can be taken as evidence of high competence (e.g., Bond, 1986, 1991). As an operationalization, a scenario was used in the interviews in which the intention was to buy a used car. In this context, the question was asked whether one would follow the recommendations of a member of a certain social category ("friend") when choosing the vehicle.

Statements of European Managers

Many European managers (especially those with a long period of residence in China) would be more likely to buy a used car from a dealer recommended to them by friends:

> *I would feel slightly safer buying a second-hand car from a salesperson whom a friend had introduced me to in person rather than from someone who is a stranger. But it is not a compelling argument if a sales agent has been introduced by somebody I know. (# 04/105)*

> *In China, if I decide to buy a used car, I would feel safer buying it from a salesperson whom a friend had introduced me to in person rather than from someone who is a stranger. Because if I know this person I believe that he would consider my interests in recommending me where to buy such a car. (# 05/124)*

> *I would feel safer buying it from a salesperson whom a friend had introduced me to in person rather than from someone who is a stranger because the salesperson probably will not try to cheat me. (# 12/153)*

> *When I desire to buy a used car, I would go to somebody I know. It's part of the well-lived network and relations in China. In such case you go through people you know. In first place you do not go through strangers. (# 22/312)*

In one interview, however, a different approach was described:

> *It doesn't matter whether the salesperson was recommended to me or whether the salesperson is a stranger. (# 20/234)*

Statements of Chinese Managers

In three interviews, Chinese executives described their intention to buy a used car from a dealer recommended by a friend:

> *Of course, I'd be more comfortable buying a used car from someone recommended by a friend or relative because I already know them for a long time and have built up trust through things we experienced together. (# 07/520)*

> *I would buy a second-hand used car through a friend. It gives me a feeling of security. If a friend recommends a car dealer to me, they must have had a good experience with this car dealer. Of course, it's better to buy from them instead of buying from a complete stranger. (# 16/701)*

> *I would feel more secure buying a second-hand used car from a friend. If you buy from a stranger, he/she might not give you all the information you need. And it's not easy to turn to him/her for help if a problem occurs in the future. A friend is more likely to tell you everything you need to know, because if he/she doesn't, your friendship could be in jeopardy. Your friend will take this into consideration. (# 29/781)*

A different approach is described in two interviews:

The cars or salespeople your friends recommend might be very good, but after you purchase the car, you might still compare the price and model elsewhere. And once you find a tiny flaw, you might start blaming your friends for deceiving you. That could damage your friendship. If you buy from a stranger, you'd make an informed choice and not blame anybody else in the future. (# 10/592)

If there turns to be a problem with the second-hand car I bought or I am unhappy with the price it's trickier to talk to an acquaintance or a friend. (# 11/613)

Résumé

The assessments of social rules and traditions associated with differentiation between in-group and out-group members reported by European managers largely agree with the assessments of Chinese managers. Differences can only be noticed in nuances. This result means that social categorizations found in China are well known to European managers and that they can adapt to them. At the same time, the statements

Table 6.3: Social categorizing and trust: Statements of European and Chinese managers on four topics.

	Guanxi		Reciprocity		Staffing in Companies		Use of Information Sources in a Car Purchase Scenario
Statements of European Managers	–	Several European managers report that people in China are prepared to provide extensive support for those they are in close relationships with.	–	The longer a social relationship lasts in China, the stronger the commitment to mutual support.	–	For European managers, giving preference to family members of someone who is already employed in a company is inconceivable.	–	Many European managers (especially those who stayed in China for a long time) would rather buy a used car from a dealer recommended to them by friends.
Statements of Chinese Managers	–	For many Chinese managers, mutual support in close social relationships is an integral part of Chinese culture.	–	People in China help one another in emergency situations, but not because of poverty.	–	For many Chinese managers, giving preference to family members of someone who is already employed in a company is inconceivable.	–	Most Chinese managers would rather buy a used car from a dealer recommended to them by friends.

made by Chinese managers in the interviews show that social categorizations, e.g., in the selection of personnel no longer have the great importance that is occasionally ascribed to them in the literature.

The results are summarized in Table 6.3.

Compliance with Social Rules and Trust

To what extent do rules and their observance in everyday situations in China contribute to interpersonal trust? Four topics were addressed in the interviews:
- compliance with contracts
- trust in the Chinese legal system
- protection of intellectual property in China
- general statements on the influence of context and rules on individual behavior

Compliance with Contracts

From the perspective of European executives, the conclusion of contractual agreements in China is often seen as a measure to build mutual trust between the contracting parties (e.g., Linggi, 2011). If the agreements are kept, then trust can develop with the result that, if cooperation is continued, there is a tendency to dispense with a written fixation of the agreements made. In the long run, trust can therefore replace contracts.

From a Chinese perspective, contracts in Western societies serve to limit the mutual exploitation of the contracting parties. In this way, a lack of mutual trust can be compensated for with the help of the law. Consequently, contracts enable the conclusion, compliance and control of economic cooperation when trust is lacking (Lin & Li, 2005; see also Chapter 2). From the Chinese point of view, on the other hand, contracts are expressions of will for future cooperation, which will be implemented to the benefit of both parties under the future conditions because sincerity (诚信, *chengxin*) is the basic moral attitude of people in Chinese culture. Therefore, detailed designs of economic contracts are not considered as necessary. From the Chinese point of view, a contract only marks the beginning of a cooperation and defines its basis. According to the Chinese understanding, the need to renegotiate under changed conditions is part of good and trusting cooperation and should not be misinterpreted as a breach of contract (e.g., Tang & Reisch, 1995).

Statements of European Managers

In general, European managers have differing views on compliance with contracts in China. Some executives believe that contracts with Chinese companies are honored by Chinese contractors. In several statements, however, doubts are becoming apparent as to whether the Chinese contractual partners will actually comply with the agreements made in existing contracts:

> *Contracts are being adhered to. It works to make sure that you have in the contract what you need. Once contracts are established, they are being adhered to. (# 04/102)*

> *I have heard and I have read that contracts in China may not be respected. Up to now I have not seen any evidence of that. (# 05/120)*

> *But things are changing in China. If I consider the last twenty years, then I would say there is a tendency, especially if you are cooperating with the big companies, that their understanding about contracts is more or less the understanding of the Western party. (# 31/487)*

> *Sometimes contracts have a vague wording, so it takes some time until there is a complete understanding of what the wording of the contract or the policy means. Certain government directives are also rather vague. Sometimes you need experts that will find out what the contract or policy actually means. (# 02/056)*

> *Mostly the Chinese companies with international interactions learned how to respect contracts. I generally have a better and better impression about contractual discipline in the business. But Chinese companies never see the importance to really discuss several details, even on a daily basis about a contract. I understand in the Chinese culture to rediscuss or saying that the contract was done two years ago, so we need to do something else now. (# 19/193)*

> *The better the relationship, the more people would follow contracts. But, if the relationship is not there and you only have a piece of paper, then you can basically forget about it. (# 23/343)*

> *In China, contracts are somewhat more naively designed and finished within short time periods. Later it turns out that the Chinese contract partners want to renegotiate the contract because they were not aware of all of its consequences or had different interpretations in mind. (# 03/083)*

> *I do not think that contracts are being adhered to and followed. That hasn't changed that much. It changed a little bit. But, generally speaking, yes, contract is contract. And a lot depends on relationship and later renegotiations. (# 20/228)*

> *In the beginning of a contract the paragraphs are very clear, but in the end of the day when the Chinese see that my advantage is too big, then they change a little bit argumentation and say, "Yes, you can say like this, but you can also say like this." Or: "I understand it a little bit different." (# 21/269)*

> *A contract is not valuable the piece of paper in China. (# 27/424)*

From the point of view of many European managers, a contract does not represent a mutually binding agreement for many Chinese business partners, but rather a declaration of intent. This understanding of the contract is actually found in statements by

Chinese managers and in this respect confirms descriptions of publications from the Western cultural area (e.g., Brahm, 1995; Chung & Sievert, 1995; Tang & Reisch, 1995):

> *In China a contract is more a symbol of a relationship. In Europe it's more, the fundamental posta-ment [= pedestal, base] of how companies are working with each other. (# 19/194)*

> *In China when you sign a contract, this contract will not be adhered to and followed. A contract in China is more or less a letter of intent. (# 31/487)*

Statements of Chinese Managers

Several Chinese managers are convinced that contracts with foreign companies are adhered to. Chinese executives often refer to such contracts as legally binding:

> *Contracts between two Chinese companies are usually performed. It's basic. Nowadays the price is high, if you breach a contract. Most people wouldn't take the risk of breaking the law, ruining their reputation, and being condemned morally. (# 13/633)*

> *Over ten years ago, we would have thought that the risk of a contract not being performed was great and would have been very cautious. But nowadays, as long as a contract is signed in accor-dance with the law, the enforcement of the contract is guaranteed. (# 16/697)*

> *Our joint venture company has its Articles of Association. Both foreign and Chinese staff have to work according to the rules. It's not a question of whether we trust them with a task or not. We have to manage our staff and do business based on the rules. (# 25/749)*

> *Whatever is agreed by both parties in the contract will also be implemented. Joint venture compa-nies also have to perform their contracts. Whether the contract is fair depends on what you want and your ability to negotiate. (# 29/774)*

These reflections contrast with statements by some Chinese managers who describe contracts as a changeable agreement or as a framework. The future developments and general conditions of a cooperation can hardly be predicted when the contract is concluded. Renegotiations can and must only take place once these developments and conditions are known. Many of the following statements correspond to the prevailing assessments of the understanding of contracts in Chinese society among many European managers:

> *Whether contracts signed by two Chinese companies, are they performed depends on the nature of the company. Less important articles in a contract are in many occasions not complied with by private firms, but the important ones are. (# 07/517)*

> *Certainly, the agreement is only a white paper, a document; the most cooperation in China is only one word, we often say: honesty. Once the agreement cannot be carried out, so we probably go to the judicial process according to the terms in the agreement. But mostly in the situation with hon-esty, agreement is just papers. (# 08/543)*

Contracts between two Chinese companies are usually performed by and large, but not to 100%. Having a signed contract is only the start of the cooperation, during which both parties might use all sorts of reasons or tactics to convince the other party to modify the contract in order to maximise their own profit. The real game starts when the other party is not willing to modify the contract. Which party is strong enough to stand the loss? Europeans would almost perform their contracts to 100%. Of course, they would also negotiate if something unexpected occurs, but it's not their intention not to perform the contract. (# 14/656)

In China, contracts are not always performed to 100%, but if the other party has a reputation for always keeping their word, or you know each other very well, an oral agreement might be able to solve all the problems. On the contrary, if you don't know the other party, a signed contract cannot guarantee anything, for it might be full of pitfalls. So, you'd have a better chance of being successful doing business with people you know well. (# 14/658)

Europeans are still better than us in contract performance in the sense that they follow the terms of the contract more strictly. Europeans on the other hand tend to stick to the original contract and do not think about amending the contract even if the circumstances have changed. (# 17/719)

Chinese people are ready to renegotiate and modify the contract when there is a change of circumstance. If nothing comes out of renegotiation, they will still perform most of the contract. (# 17/719)

Chinese people need a contract when they are doing business, but they don't usually negotiate in such detail like Europeans do. We only use the contract as a foundation for our co-operation. We will try to perform the contract, but if problems occur in the process, we will renegotiate the terms. (# 18/737)

Trust in the Chinese Legal System

Statements of European Managers

During the interviews, each manager was asked to state his trust in the Chinese legal system. Most of the European managers are critical of the Chinese legal system. A positive development of the Chinese legal system is seen, however, in a few statements by European executives:

I would not say that in China, the legal system can be trusted. But I can say that the legal system is a solid system in China. I think it's a good system. But the enforcement of the legal system is many times compromised. So, you can see the written law which is very helpful, which is very protective, but whenever enforcement is coming to the picture, you never know how it goes. My impression is that in China sometimes legal questions can be interpreted based on political truth and based on corruption, based on a lot of other things, so I believe that it is a nice legal system which is there, but many things are happening differently in the background. (# 19/195)

In China, the legal system can not be trusted in the same way as we're used to in Europe. In China, we do not have the same separation of powers. And thus, the legal power is different to see than in Europe. And this you can see when you go down the lines and when it really comes to lawsuits or whatever disputes. (# 22/309)

I would not want to come into the situation that I have to test whether the legal system in China can be trusted. (# 23/344)

In China, the legal system can maybe not as much trusted as in Western countries. Because the legal system isn't that developed. And of course, this has also influence on your right of property. (# 26/392)

In principle, I would say yes, the legal system can be trusted. But many things are not clearly defined. So, in Chinese law there is quite often a possibility of interpretation. (# 31/489)

The legal system in China can be seen as work in progress. It is not perfect. (# 04/103)

Two European managers complained that foreigners are discriminated by the Chinese legal system:

I do not think that in China, the legal system can be trusted. I wouldn't believe that if I had a conflict with a Chinese party and using the legal system, I don't think I will have a fair chance. Reports from people who have been in conflict situations quite clearly state that there is a general bias towards the local population and against foreigners and there is also corruption. So, whoever can find a way to get to a certain judge will receive favourable rulings, whereas the other party will not. I think the rule of law generally is not very strong in China. (# 20/228)

Even within the law, there are differences between foreigners and Chinese people whenever it comes to taxation or labour law. For example, the labour law, when a foreigner is terminated from companies, for the Chinese people there are laws that are actually implemented. Whereas for foreigners, we are expected to take care of ourselves much more. (# 20/229)

In China, the legal system cannot be trusted. If you go to arbitration when you have a contract, you definitely as a foreign company you will not get any advantage or even the law. This is not a neutral system. In a dispute [between our company and our state-owned joint venture partner company] definitely the judge that should be neutral will not be neutral. (# 27/425)

In two interviews, the doubts about the Chinese legal system expressed by European managers are explained by imprecise wording in the laws:

In principle, I would say yes, the legal system can be trusted. But many things are not clearly defined. So, in Chinese law there is quite often a possibility of interpretation. (# 31/489)

The legal system in China cannot be trusted. It's too flexible. It gives not enough orientation to the people; not enough safety and security. (# 12/150)

Statements of Chinese Managers

Many Chinese managers have a high level of trust in the Chinese legal system:

I would totally agree if someone says that the legal system in China could be trusted. Our legal system is well developed and suits China the best. (# 10/589)

I agree that the Chinese legal system is trustworthy. People are more and more law-abiding. The anti-corruption project has also been successful. In the past, some government officials interfered in legal affairs, but that has changed. Our government takes it very seriously and the legal environment is fairer now. (# 15/679)

I believe we have a sound legal system in China. (# 25/761)

We have a relatively sound legal system in China. (# 16/696)

However, several statements by Chinese managers indicate that weaknesses in the Chinese legal system are being perceived:

It is not unusual that a Chinese government official has made a promise and then is replaced by someone else, and the new official won't or can't keep that promise anymore, probably because of a change in the market. In this case you can't ask the government for compensation. Europeans have more faith in governments' promises. (# 15/668)

The Chinese legal system is being improved over time. Of course, the legal system in China is not perfect, it has a lot of problems to solve. My opinion is that the Chinese legal system still has a lot of room for improvement. (# 09/569)

However, many Chinese managers emphasize that the Chinese legal system is in a process of continuous development. This process is mostly rated positively:

If somebody says that Chinese legal system deserves to be relied on, I agree with this point, China is a state of ceremonies. Chinese rules and laws are continuously in improvement. And there are laws to abide by. (# 08/544)

The Chinese legal system is trustworthy. It is developed on the basis of the civil law system, but also drew lessons from the common law system. The law is being revised regularly and the interpretation of the law is updated every year. So, our legal system is being improved continuously. (# 13/633)

I agree that the Chinese legal system is reliable. The legal system has improved a lot and people are more and more law-abiding. (# 29/779)

The legal system in mainland China is improving, but it still has a long way to go until it reaches the level of European legal systems. (# 11/610)

The Chinese legal system is undergoing continuous improvement. It is okay to trust the Chinese legal system when you're familiar with it and practice business basing on a good understanding of it. (# 14/657)

There is a continuous improvement of the Chinese legal system. It is a lot better than it was five or ten years ago, and I'm convinced that it will be a lot better in five or ten years than it is now. (# 30/797)

The difference between the Chinese legal culture and the European legal tradition is seen as an advantage by several Chinese managers:

In life, we have to obey the law. On top of that, we will deal with things in different ways based on the circumstances. (# 17/719)

China is a society of relationships, where human relationships are often more important than rules. Chinese people usually put relationships first, as long as it's not a serious breach of the law. Europeans might put rules first. Europeans are better at complying with the rules. (# 29/778)

Protection of Material and Intellectual Property in China

Statements of European Managers

In four interviews with European managers, insufficient protection of property, especially intellectual property, is complained about:

There is a lot of uncertainty around intellectual property and real physical ownership of things. From that point of view, you can say in China the property of individuals is not protected. (# 04/102)

I believe in China the government has the right to take away anything they want to, or they find a way to take away anything they want to. In this respect in China, definitely a lot is in the hand of the government from the system, and they can take away things much easier than, for example, in Europe. (# 19/192)

You can't say for sure that in China the property of individuals is protected. I think it applies to the actual status of the national law. I think the national law makes in the first place the protection of property quite clear. When it comes to intellectual property rights, I'm quite aware that this is not yet a well protected country. (# 22/308)

In China, the property of individuals is not protected. You see it when China government wants to build a railway. They come, take you out of your house and build the railway straight through it. Probably you'll get another house elsewhere but first, you lose your house where you were born in. So, there is no protection in my opinion. (# 27/424)

The following passage is found in an interview with a European manager, in which the respondent gives an example of how the Chinese legal system protects property:

I would say that in China the property of individuals is protected. We learnt about stories that land was taken from farmers when there were big projects of the state, so in this case, the property is not protected. But these are single cases which are exceptions. In general, I would say that the property of individuals is protected today in China. (# 31/486)

Improvements in the protection of property by the Chinese legal system are recognized by two European managers:

In China, the property of individuals is protected to an extent. Although there is a law on paper, the protection depends on where you live and it depends on circumstances, e.g., the new credit system. (# 01/027)

In mainland China, intellectual property seems to be better protected in more recent times. Even court cases recently were finished in favour of companies which found their IP [intellectual property] violated. China's intention seems to be to step up in the value chain, away from being just a manufacturing plant of the world to generate own innovations. (# 03/082)

Statements of Chinese Managers

Many Chinese managers take property protection for granted. The relevant interview passages show that all of these statements refer to material property:

I think that in China private property is protected. Now in China, the laws and regulations are quite sane. China is a safe country with strict order. Most ordinary people have a high index of happiness. (# 08/543)

I think that personal property is under protection in China. My personal property has never been subject to or under the threat of any damages. (# 14/656)

In China any lawful property is protected. Illegal property on the contrary is not protected. It could be seized by the court. (# 15/678)

As far as I know, for us ordinary people, our personal property is being protected. What we earn through work is not under any threat. (# 25/760)

However, some Chinese managers question the protection of intellectual and material property by the Chinese legal system:

If you buy a house in China, you might appear to be the owner of the house, but you don't actually own the land your house is sitting on; instead, you obtain rights to use the land for up to 70 years. So, in this sense I think the protection is not enough. (# 09/568)

Intellectual property protection is a big problem in my opinion. The Europeans are now aware that China is not doing particularly well in this aspect. Plagiarism remains a large obstacle to building trust between the two sides, and we need to ease their worries, if we want a smooth cooperation in the future. (# 09/576)

There are risks when you think about it, but it doesn't happen that often in real life that personal property is not protected in China. (# 13/633)

I doubt whether private property is protected in China. Given the chance, I would put my property somewhere else than in mainland China. There are more risks here than in foreign countries or Hong Kong, because of the constant change of policy. The market is subject to too many regulations from the government. (# 11/610)

Influence of Context and Rules on Behavior

In order to collect statements on this topic, the respondents were asked to comment on the statement, "Do you think that in China, the behavior of most people depends on the situation or is it more influenced by established rules?"

Statements of European Managers

According to many European managers, the individual behavior of the Chinese is more influenced by rules than by the situational context:

> In China, the behaviour of most people is definitely based on established rules. (# 02/056)

> In mainland China, the behaviour of most people is more influenced by established rules. (# 03/081)

> I think that the rules inside China companies are more complex and more hard than in Germany. The status of managers, leaders, is very important, totally important. In China I never see that someone who is lower in the company will ask something. They even will never ask or meet these other people at a very high level. (# 21/265)

> The integration into rules and regulations, I think, is in China slightly higher than in Europe. Rules and regulations apply much more to people who are influenced by their social surrounding, also within the company. Rules and regulations have a higher impact than in the Western world, I think. (# 22/307)

However, the statements of two European managers indicate a different assessment:

> For private family life, there are strong rules for every behaviour, every relation. Looking on business it's more and more a global business attitude, it's more and more comparable to that what we have here in Europe or North America. (# 28/456)

> My impression is that the behaviour of most people depends more on the situation than on rules and regulations. (# 19/190)

Statements of Chinese Managers

According to most Chinese managers, rules and the situational context have a similarly high influence on the individual behavior of Chinese people:

> In China, in big cities the rules play a bigger role, whereas in small towns the circumstances have bigger influences on people's behaviours. (# 11/609)

> China is a society of relationships, where human relationships are often more important than rules. Chinese people usually put relationships first, as long as it's not a serious breach of the law. Europeans might put rules first. Europeans are better at complying with the rules. (# 29/778)

> Foreigners might be under the impression that Chinese people have a lot of rules, traditions, or social conventions to follow. But China has changed a lot. Our society is getting younger. Young people are challenging traditional rules and conventions. Also, there is a great disparity between first-tier cities and small towns. Young people in Beijing, Shanghai, or Guangzhou will give you very different answers to this question compared to young people from a small town. (# 30/796)

> Young Chinese people from a first-tier city are probably more inclined to make decisions on the basis of the circumstances, logic, and their own knowledge. A person from a small town is more likely to follow the rules that have already existed in their environment for some time. (# 30/797)

In one interview with a Chinese manager, a different assessment is formulated:

> *You need to follow these rules, otherwise you won't be able to achieve anything in this society. You need to forge ahead sailing the course of laws and regulations. That's the starting point. Morality and reason come after that. (# 13/632)*

Résumé
European and Chinese managers express very different views about the influence of rules on individual behavior in Chinese culture. At the same time, however, it should also be noted that the managers unanimously report on developments that could lead to a more uniform understanding of laws and contracts.

The importance of rules for individual behavior in China is judged inconsistently. European managers complain about a lack of compliance with the legal system, law and rules. Chinese managers emphasize the importance of rules for individual behavior, but often point out that context also influences behavior.

Trust in the Chinese legal system and the protection of property in China are rated more positively by Chinese managers than by European managers. Recent improvements are emphasized by Chinese managers; they are acknowledged by some European managers.

Overall, European and Chinese managers have differing opinions on compliance with contracts. The Chinese understanding of contracts as declarations of intent, which in individual cases must always result in new negotiations and agreements, is also understood by some European managers, in some cases, sympathetically.

Overall, the assessments of European and Chinese managers are different in this area. However, the assessments of Chinese and European managers seem to be converging. The results are summarized in Table 6.4.

Role Expectations and Trust

Only a few interview passages can be found in which a reference is made to the role expectations of the managers involved. The few relevant interview passages can be assigned to the following three topics:
– behavior in hierarchical relationships
– separation of business relationships and private relationships
– *guanxi.*

Table 6.4: Social rules and trust: Statements of European and Chinese managers on four topics.

	Compliance with Contracts	Trust in the Chinese Legal System	Protection of Intellectual Property in China	Influence of Context and Rules on Individual Behavior
Statements of European Managers	– Compliance with contracts in China is assessed inconsistently by European managers. – From the perspective of many European managers, for many Chinese business partners a contract represents a declaration of intent.	– Trust in the Chinese legal system is mostly assessed as low. – Discrimination against foreigners is feared or complained about. – Imprecise wording in laws is complained about.	– Inadequate protection of property, especially intellectual property, is often complained about by European managers. – Improvements in the protection of property are recognized by many European managers.	– For most European managers, rules in China have a greater influence on behavior than the situational context.
Statements of Chinese Managers	– Many Chinese managers are convinced that contracts with foreign companies are honored. They are often referred to as legally binding. – Many Chinese managers describe contracts as agreements and frameworks within which renegotiations can or must take place.	– Trust in the Chinese legal system is mostly assessed as high. – The continuous development of the Chinese legal system is viewed predominantly as positive. – Imprecise wordings in Chinese legal texts are sometimes viewed as an advantage.	– The protection of property is taken for granted by many Chinese managers. – Occasionally doubts are expressed about the protection of property in China.	– For most Chinese managers, rules and the situational context have a similar influence on individual behavior.

Behavior in Hierarchical Relationships

Statements of European Managers
Several European managers describe the behavior of their Chinese colleagues in the presence of superiors. They find that in meetings when senior managers are present, employees from lower hierarchical levels are hardly willing to contribute to discussions. This behavior is described particularly clearly in the following passage:

> If they are a little bit higher positioned, they tell something, they give some suggestions. But if they are not very high, if they are not third degree inside of the organigram, then they prefer not to talk too much inside of the meeting because they think, "Okay, I will not say this because my boss is here, my boss is there, so I prefer to say nothing and be quiet." They are not really participating, everyone in the same way. It depends, if you are a little bit higher, then you say more. If you are a little bit lower, then you will be quiet. (# 21/257)

Statements of Chinese Managers
Statements by Chinese managers confirm the observations reported by European managers. The Chinese managers point out that you can exchange ideas with colleagues at the same hierarchical level without any problems, but that you have to be obedient to superiors:

> You could be more easy-going while talking to people at your own level or below your level, while you need to listen more to your superiors, because of their personalities, for example they might like to have everything under their control. (# 11/597)

Separation of Business Relationships and Private Relationships

Statements of European Managers
One European manager expressed his impression that, for Chinese colleagues, building a friendship is also a prerequisite for settling contracts in business relationships. This means that managers from different cultural backgrounds should not restrict self-perception to the role of a manager in business negotiations and agreement settling:

> In China, you trust more in people that you know than in people you do not know. If you know someone, and you do a contract, and you know this people, and you know the family of this people or you know someone who knows this people, then it's much easier than if you are a total new face for him, because one thing I learned here is: First you make friendship and then you make a contract. You can never make this different. (# 21/271)

Statements of Chinese Managers

One interview provides insights into how Chinese managers understand their role in business relationships. According to him, mutual trust is not important in negotiations and the settlement of contracts. Instead, common interests, which are essential for successful cooperation, are emphasized:

> *For businessmen, trust is not that relevant. What we try to achieve is a win–win co--operation.* (# 25/761)

Guanxi

Statements of European Managers

Only a few statements by European managers can be found on this topic. According to this, the Chinese only behave in a trustworthy and helpful manner within their *guanxi* network of relationships:

> *The parental relationship is extremely important. They are supporting each other in their own guanxi. In their guanxi they are really supporting. But outside their guanxi, they are not very helpful to each other. Maybe they are more ignorant to people who don't belong to their guanxi.* (# 19/180)

Statements on this topic could not be found in the interviews with Chinese managers.

Résumé

The few indications of the importance of roles for trust that can be found in the interviews concern the rather high-power distance in hierarchical relationships that applies in China, the importance of building positive personal relationships as a prerequisite for successful negotiations and the settlement of contracts and the importance of *guanxi* in everyday life.

The importance of trust in business relationships is not seen uniformly. Few European managers consider trust to be an important prerequisite for business relationships, whereas few Chinese managers consider common interests to be an important prerequisite for successful cooperation.

Overall, the statements on this area show a considerable degree of agreement (see Table 6.5). References to the cultural dimensions of individualism/collectivism, power distance and specific versus diffuse cultures formulated by Hofstede and Trompenaars can be seen.

Table 6.5: Social roles and trust: Statements of European and Chinese managers on three topics.

	Behaviour in Hierarchical Relationships		Separation of Business Relationships and Private Relationships		*Guanxi*
Statements of European Managers	–	When senior managers are present, subordinates in China tend not to dare to speak up.	–	For Chinese managers, building a friendship is a prerequisite for concluding contracts in business relationships.	–	Chinese people behave in a trustworthy and helpful manner only within their *guanxi* network of relationships.
Statements of Chinese Managers	–	You can easily communicate with colleagues at the same level in the hierarchy, and you have to follow higher-up people of higher levels.	–	In business relationships, trust is not important. Here, common interests count for the success of the cooperation.		

Dispositional Trust

Dispositional trust means the general, situation- and person-independent willingness of an individual to place a certain amount of trust in interaction partners. What dispositional trust do respondents bring to their business activities? What dispositional trust do they attribute to their business partners? The statements of the respondents can be assigned to two subject areas:
– perception of the risk of European companies and managers of being cheated in China
– perceived self-interest of the Chinese

Perception of the Risk of European Companies and their Managers of Being Cheated in China

Statements of European Managers
Some European managers see a rather high risk of being cheated in China. With regard to Chinese people, a dispositional distrust seems to emerge:

> *In a JV I felt I had to be very vigilant because you never have 100% trust because the parties' interests are not wholly identical.* (# 01/004)

> *In China nowadays, you must be alert because otherwise someone may take advantage of you; this is what each Chinese sometimes calls wisdom. I call it the lie of cheating. So, I do not want to be tricked by the Chinese wisdom. (# 19/187)*

According to the assessment of some European managers, the risk of being cheated in European–Chinese joint ventures is reduced if all partners are pursuing common goals:

> *For us sometimes, it is an issue in the joint venture to combine goals, to have on our side more of a culture-oriented "trustship," but to see that our joint venture partner is very much oriented to a control culture. (# 31/473)*

In one interview, a European manager said that, from his point of view, the intentions of the Chinese are difficult to figure out. This impairs the general tendency to trust Chinese business partners:

> *I would generally agree with the statement that in China nowadays you must be alert because otherwise someone may take advantage of you. It is because you don't know if the intentions of all people you deal with are genuine. In China, people try not to show in public what their intentions are. (# 05/119)*

Statements of Chinese Managers

Several Chinese managers see a rather high risk of being cheated when doing business in China. Against this background, their attribution of dispositional trust among the Chinese appears to be rather weak:

> *You can only trust people to a certain degree. There is sometimes a conflict of interest. You can't trust them completely unless you've known them very well over time. Personally, I don't think I can trust anybody 100%. (# 11/608)*

> *It is true that in today's China, you need to stay alert in order not to be taken advantage of. Chinese people grow up in a highly competitive environment, they need to employ all kinds of measures to achieve their goals all the time, which includes using your relationship with your colleagues or their mistakes. (# 14/654)*

> *Of course, in the case of conflict of interest, some people might turn out not to be so good. We need to rely on our own judgment and spend more time with people we are friendly with, keep our distance from people if there is a conflict of interest or a feeling of estrangement. (# 17/718)*

> *I agree with the statement that in today's China, you need to stay alert in order not to be taken advantage of. You have to be cautious when you're doing business. Chinese people place too much emphasis on controlling costs. When you are doing business with the Chinese, sometimes you're forced to accept a price lower than your cost. As long as you're doing business, you have to face the problem of being under constant pressure to lower your cost. (# 18/735)*

> *Chinese people are generally quite clever, but lack a long-term vision, in the sense that they are mostly concerned with things in front of them, and not things in the future. Chinese people have a*

strong desire to fight for resources. With so many people and so few resources, they are possibly more selfish than people elsewhere. A good quality of Chinese people is their diligence. I have a lot of friends who work between 10 to 12 hours per day. (# 07/514)

Two Chinese managers estimate that the risk of being cheated when doing business with the Chinese is rather high if the personal interests of Chinese persons are involved:

When their own interest is not involved, most Chinese people could be trusted. But once their own interest is involved, they're likely to give priority to their own interest and forget about the company's interest. (# 14/654)

You can only trust people to a certain degree. There is sometimes a conflict of interest. You can't trust them completely unless you've known them very well over time. Personally, I don't think I can trust anybody 100%. (# 11/608)

According to some Chinese managers interviewed, it is often impossible to find out what the Chinese really think and intend:

I think Europeans are more trustworthy in most cases, because they don't keep their thoughts hidden. They'd tell you if they have a problem with you, unlike the Chinese. The Chinese might not say anything to your face, even if they have something against you for fear of losing face [面子, mianzi] or perhaps in order to save your face, or simply because they are of a lower status. It's impossible to know what they really think. A Chinese person might appear to be a very close friend of yours, but they would still keep a lot of thoughts secret from you. (# 14/655)

Perceived Self-interest of the Chinese

Statements of European Managers
A European manager concludes from the behavior observed among the Chinese that, from his point of view, the Chinese can act quite unexpectedly in an egoistic, self-interested manner:

It was a very big surprise to me that my Chinese colleagues are very egoistic. What I observe is a high degree of egoism, in the company but also outside the company in the social environment of people. (# 03/076)

This European manager reports on experiences according to which the Chinese use ambiguities in the regulation of legally relevant issues to their own advantage:

In China I very often have the feeling that if there is a hole in the regulation, then people read it and decide that it is up to them to interpret this to their own benefit and are then acting in an egoistic way. (# 03/078)

Because in China people tend to interpret vague rules and regulations to their own benefit and then are acting in an egoistic way, foreigners might feel being cheated. (# 03/078)

Statements of Chinese Managers

Two Chinese managers point out that the Chinese experience a lot of competitive situations in their socialization, which is why they are used to exploiting the weaknesses and mistakes of others. Therefore, dispositional trust among the Chinese should be rather low:

> It is true that in today's China, you need to stay alert in order not to be taken advantage of. Chinese people grow up in a highly competitive environment; they need to employ all kinds of measures to achieve their goals all the time, which includes using your relationship with your colleagues or their mistakes. (# 14/654)

> Chinese people are generally quite clever, but lack a long-term vision, in the sense that they are mostly concerned with things in front of them, and not things in the future. Chinese people have a strong desire to fight for resources. With so many people and so few resources, they are possibly more selfish than people elsewhere. A good quality of Chinese people is their diligence. I have a lot of friends who work between 10 to 12 hours per day. (# 07/514)

From the point of view of one Chinese manager, the Chinese can very well be trusted, because they act in a harmonious and emotional manner when it comes to complying with the law:

> The Chinese believe in harmony and the virtue of moderation [中庸, zhongyong]. Europeans are direct and like maintaining order. Chinese people show more feelings, whereas Europeans are better at obeying rules. (# 10/585)

Résumé

European and Chinese managers alike believe that general trust in China tends to be low. Both the Chinese and the Europeans rate the risk of being cheated in China as rather high, especially when the persons involved do not pursue common interests or when the Chinese have their own interests involved.

The self-interest orientation of the Chinese is perceived by all managers as rather pronounced. While the European managers mostly leave it at that, some of the Chinese managers point to the competitive situation that is typical for socialization of the Chinese. They also point out that the Chinese often rely on their self-interest in legally ambiguous situations.

Overall, China is seen as a country in which a high level of general trust should be rather out of place.

The results of this section are summarized in Table 6.6.

Table 6.6: Dispositional trust: Statements of European and Chinese managers on two topics.

	Perception of the Risk of European Companies and Managers of Being Cheated in China	Perceived Self-Interest of the Chinese
Statements of European Managers	– Some European managers see a rather high risk of being taken advantage of in China. – In joint ventures, the risk of being taken advantage of can be reduced if all actors pursue common goals. – Chinese people's intentions are difficult to figure out.	– Chinese people tend to behave in an unexpectedly selfish and self-interested manner. – Chinese people tend to exploit ambiguities in the regulation of legally relevant issues to their own advantage.
Statements of Chinese Managers	– Many Chinese managers see a rather high risk of being taken advantage of in China. – The risk of being taken advantage of is greater when personal interests of Chinese persons are involved. – It is often impossible to find out what Chinese people really think and intend.	– Chinese people frequently experience competitive situations in their socialization, which is why they are used to exploiting other people's weaknesses and mistakes. – Chinese people are more sensitive to their feelings when it comes to complying with law and order.

7 Discussion and Implications

The Results in Review

The appraisal of recent studies on joint venture research has shown that trust is a key success factor in promoting economic cooperation. In essence, joint ventures are cooperative relationships in which one cooperation partner (the trustor) expects a benefit from the other cooperation partner (the trustee). However, the trustor cannot be certain that this result will actually occur. Trust describes the expectation of the trustor that the trustee will actually show behavior that leads to the hoped-for benefit. The aspect of risk is widely ignored in reliance on receiving this benefit. Of course, this trusting is mutual, so that both parties are engaged in trusting to other to deliver on their hoped-for benefits.

The literature review also revealed that trust is mostly understood as a cognitive phenomenon. Three characteristics ascribed to cooperation partners form the cognitive dimensions of trust: their benevolence, their integrity and their abilities to deliver on the hoped-for outcomes. Only a few years ago, affective-emotional aspects of trust and cultural differences in the processes of building and maintaining trust also came into the focus of trust research. For trust research, which is largely dominated by authors from Western cultures, these new aspects are of great importance. Here, however, a considerable research desideratum becomes apparent, because theories of interpersonal trust and empirical work on these aspects from non-Western cultural areas are difficult to access and can therefore only be found sporadically in the relevant literature.

The continued existence and further development of economic cooperation between Chinese and European companies will largely depend on the mutual trust that has been built up and can be maintained between the organizations and people involved. The present study contributes to gaining insights into processes of trust building and maintenance and to deriving recommendations that can contribute to the establishment of new as well as to the strengthening of existing European–Chinese economic relations.

The most important finding of this study, in agreement with numerous relevant studies, is that trust is a universal, i.e., a cross-cultural phenomenon. Confucius already emphasized trust in one another more than 2500 years ago: "Trust is the most important thing for a person" (Kong & Legge, 2009). Many of the statements made by the Chinese and European managers we interviewed show how important trust is for the success of intercultural business partnerships. In addition, both the theoretical considerations and the statements made by the managers interviewed indicate that the cognitive and affective-emotional structural characteristics of trust show significant similarities in the national cultures considered. This also applies to the four con-

https://doi.org/10.1515/9783111344560-007

textual factors of social categorization, roles played, rules in social interactions and dispositional trust considered in the conceptual framework.

However, the cross-cultural similarities in the understanding of trust must not obscure the fact that culture-specific differences between Germany and China must be taken into account when weighting the cognitive and affective components of trust along with the relevance of context factors.

Relevance of Affective Trust in the Chinese Culture

The results of the present study draw particular attention to the importance of affective trust in the Chinese culture. One of the common stereotypes about people from China, often found in Western cultures, is their characterization as emotionally controlled. Social harmony and saving face are considered important rules for social interaction. In consequence, Europeans and Americans find it quite difficult to correctly perceive and interpret the feelings and preferences of Chinese colleagues. The results of the present study show that expectation asymmetries, misunderstandings and misinterpretations can occur on the level of affective trust: Many European managers working in China refuse to enter into social contacts with their Chinese colleagues that go beyond the relationships at work. Conversely, many Chinese managers would like to have closer, more intensive contacts with European colleagues beyond the situation at work. This disconnect is regrettable, since there are clear indications that, from a Chinese perspective, these closer social contacts can be an important basis for building mutual trust. Some European managers see a common cultural basis as a prerequisite for functioning social contacts with Chinese colleagues, but at the same time prevent such a basis from forming by rejecting social contacts outside of the workplace.

This result can be interpreted as an indication that managers working abroad are repeatedly called upon to examine their expectations, assumptions and perceptions to determine the extent to which they follow their cultural stereotypes. In particular, managers from other cultures should be prepared during their stay abroad in China to discover that the widespread stereotype of the allegedly emotionally controlled and distant Chinese is only superficially correct. Signs of interest on the part of Chinese colleagues in social contacts with European colleagues beyond the work environment can be interpreted as indications that the Chinese colleagues are striving to establish a trusting relationship.

A further recommendation for action in this context is that Western managers should exercise restraint in expressing their feelings during their stays in China. From the perspective of the Chinese involved, the open display of negative feelings in particular can mean a loss of face for both parties involved and should be carefully avoided.

Components of Cognitive Trust

Among the surprising findings of this study are asymmetries in trust between Chinese and European executives. They are particularly evident in the components of cognitive trust. The Chinese managers credit their European colleagues with a high level of integrity, great benevolence and most of those skills that are needed to get the job done. On the other hand, European managers mistrust their Chinese colleagues when it comes to their benevolence and integrity. European managers also see certain deficits in the professional competence of their Chinese colleagues.

Could the finding that Chinese managers attribute high benevolence and integrity to their European colleagues represent a social desirability effect? This effect describes the fact that respondents tend to give answers in interviews that they expect the interviewer will evaluate positively. However, the relevant sections of the interviews do not reveal that Chinese managers only made statements in the sense of a social desirability effect. Rather, the corresponding assessments in several interviews are supplemented by descriptions of personal experiences and thus substantiated.

From the observed trust asymmetries, negative consequences for trust building between European and Chinese executives can be deduced. Recognizing and correctly understanding mutual behavioral expectations is of great importance for building trust in business relationships. However, many statements made in the interviews indicate that the behavior expectations of the respective cooperation partners are largely misperceived by both European and Chinese executives. It is possible and even probable that this asymmetry will result in disappointments that can have a significant negative impact on the quality of the relationship as it develops. Disruptions in trust building would be the result. This concern applies equally to the three components of cognitive trust (benevolence, integrity, and ability).

Therefore, it is to be feared that economic cooperation in European–Chinese joint ventures and other forms of cooperation will be exposed to permanent strains, since Chinese executives in particular can repeatedly be disappointed in their expectations about their European colleagues. Trust is difficult to build in such strained relationships.

To improve this situation, recommendations for action are primarily aimed at the European managers, who tend to be very suspicious of economic cooperation with Chinese participants. European managers should be more open and attentive when working with Chinese executives. They should also be more responsive to Chinese managers' expectations regarding the three cognitive trust components. An approach that Chinese actors use in such situations may be appropriate here: willingness to trust and vulnerability are initially used in situations with manageable risk. If the new cooperation partner proves to be sufficiently trustworthy, the cooperation can be carefully expanded in further steps. If, on the other hand, the cooperation leads to unexpected, negative results, the trust in the Chinese cooperation partners would have to be readjusted and perhaps re-negotiated.

Social Categorizing

It should also be taken into account that for Chinese actors when entering into new economic relationships, categorical trust[1] is much more important than the dispositional trust of the individual. The task for European managers is to create a basis of trust across the hierarchy through frequent contact and intensive communication with employees at as many levels of the company as possible. This strategy will work better if European managers respond to Chinese culture and accommodate to it.

Good Chinese language skills on the part of European managers support this effect, because it allows them to express that they appreciate Chinese culture and are interested in understanding by meeting its challenging language. Several interview statements and the entrepreneurial experiences of one member of the team of authors show that language skills are a key to accessing Chinese culture and society and are viewed by Chinese cooperation partners as an indicator of interest in and commitment to Chinese culture.

Sociological and social psychological analyses of Chinese culture and society unanimously show the great importance of social categorization. Within certain social categories (family, relatives, friends, friends of relatives, people of the same regional origin), benevolent behavior dominates, because it can improve one's own or one's own family's reputation and relational credit within these social categories. The trustworthiness acquired in this way becomes an important factor for social standing within the groups mentioned. Conversely, breaches of trust usually damage social standing and can result in a loss of trust. This will very likely strain the network of relationships within these social categories.

Foreign business partners do not initially fall into one of the aforementioned social categories of Chinese society. At least in the early phases of a business partnership, they initially belong to the category of strangers. However, they have the opportunity to gain access to desired social categories. There are two ways to do so:

- The foreigner has proven to be a trustworthy partner in long-term business relationships. This usually time-consuming process of building trust can be accelerated if the foreign manager shows great interest in Chinese cultural history in its many forms and develops an understanding of this rich legacy and the Chinese value system.
- The foreigner has already earned a high reputation as a trustworthy business partner in another context and is recommended to third parties by a Chinese manager. In this way, access to social categories in Chinese society is made easier for foreign managers and access to corresponding *guanxi* relationships[2] is accelerated.

---

1 See Chapter 4.
2 See Chapter 4.

Access to and staying in social categories and *guanxi* networks requires compliance with social rules. In this context, trust in people also means trust in the social rules that apply within certain social categories. The interest in maintaining one's reputation, which is an important prerequisite for access to *guanxi* networks, acts as an incentive to cultivate one's own trustworthiness. Knowledge of these social rules and their appropriate application to various social categorizations is essential for the professional success of foreign executives in China.

Confirmed Expectations and Surprises

What study results did the authors expect? Expectations have been confirmed in some aspects, while there have been surprises in other areas.

Perhaps the most surprising finding is that the asymmetries in the cognitive components of trust between European and Chinese executives were not expected to be that striking. Further studies will have to examine whether these trust asymmetries are reflected in more European–Chinese economic cooperations and how these asymmetries will develop in the future.

Second, the Chinese managers' assessments of a generally rather low level of German or European workers' diligence were not expected. This weak impression does not correspond to the self-image of Germans and Europeans that has prevailed for decades. Meanwhile, in Germany, too, an assessment is spreading that the willingness of Germans to work hard is tending to decrease.

Third, some statements made by Chinese executives in interviews reveal an attitude that can be interpreted as an expression of a "New Chinese Self-Confidence." References to the growing importance of Chinese values and achievements go hand in hand with clear criticism of Western values and motives.

A look at China's history and the relations between China and the Western colonial powers can help to explain this new self-confidence. The treatment of China by the colonial powers up until the 19th century had a negative impact on Chinese self-confidence for many decades. China's economic and social decline in the early 20th century also contributed to China's negative self-image. A counter-movement began with the founding of the Chinese Republic in the mid-20th century. The resurgence of China's economy thanks to Deng Xiao Ping's opening-up policy, prompted by his call to "Enrich yourself!" has led to a significant increase in the wealth of the Chinese people, especially those of the upper and middle classes. In addition, the fact that poverty has been largely eliminated in the country fills the Chinese population with pride. China's growing economic and political position in the world is also boosting national self-confidence. As our study shows, this increased self-confidence can also be observed in the business behavior of many Chinese executives.

Some of their interview statements indicate that the Chinese economy and society are believed to have attained a high degree of technological and social superiority.

Several statements by the managers interviewed are also permeated by a pronounced sense of nationalism. These tendencies can be explained in accordance with the teaching of Confucius, who declared self-improvement to be the greatest value.[3] Chinese nationalism and the assessment of the superiority of the Chinese system strengthen and underpin the already typical social categorizations in Chinese society. They contribute to the clear separation between in-group and out-group. European leaders will find themselves increasingly exposed to this nationalism in the future. It may be possible to counter it, if respect is shown towards Chinese culture and, in particular, China's rapid and successful fight against poverty is acknowledged. This respect should be duly and often expressed, especially in public forums.

Fourth, changes in staffing procedures at Chinese companies have surprised us. Various publications from the turn of the millennium pointed out that decisions about filling vacancies in Chinese companies took into account family and friendly relationships with those already employed in the company. At the same time, employees tried to accommodate their family members and friends in the company. This shows a nepotism that is still widespread in collectivist cultures. It illustrates that in these cultures trust is placed in strangers according to their membership in certain social categories. At the same time, a mostly patriarchal management style makes companies particularly attractive employers if members of the same social category are already employed there.

However, the interview statements of many Chinese executives show a changing picture and contradict the recruitment practices mentioned in the literature and also confirm the experiences of the authors. The procedure described by the Chinese managers, which primarily depends on the professional competence of applicants, can be viewed as an example of so-called Chinese individualism, which is permeated by collectivist traits. This Chinese variant of individualism seems to be trending as multinational literature emerges. In the coming years it will have to be examined whether this trend will continue to strengthen.

Fifth, the assessment by Chinese executives that the Chinese suspect a lack of benevolence in business relationships with one another has come as a surprise. The self-image of the Chinese and the assessments of European executives seem to correspond in this regard. A possible explanation for the lack of benevolence feared by the majority of Chinese and the associated self-interest orientation of the Chinese could be that most Chinese have been exposed to extreme competition in many areas of life since childhood. This could promote and strengthen the self-interest seeking of the Chinese.

Sixth, the mostly positive comments by Chinese executives on the Chinese legal system have come as a surprise. From a Western point of view, the vagueness of many rules in the Chinese legal system is often criticized – some of the European managers we interviewed joined in this critique. This vagueness creates room for in-

---

3 See Chapter 3.

terpretation, making legal disputes at a Chinese court that follows an adjudicatory process a risk that is difficult to calculate. From a Western point of view, the quality of a legal system is measured by the clarity of legal terms, regulations and the assessment of sanctions. The more flexible these components of a legal system are designed to be, the less confidence individuals from Western national cultures have in the legal system. From the Chinese point of view, the flexibility of the Chinese legal system is even an advantage, because it allows the judges to assess the individual case when applying legal provisions and thus respond more flexibly in the application of legal provisions to present circumstances.

It is here that differences between the members of Western cultures and the Chinese culture with regard to their tolerance of ambiguity become apparent. From a Chinese perspective, the perception of ambiguity in legal regulations could even be seen as an advantage because it corresponds to the principles of Daoism.[4] This principle invites flexible interpretations of regulations and favors a pragmatic approach by decision-makers.

The positive assessments of the Chinese legal system were also surprising because many Chinese tend to reject the use of law and social order to settle conflicts and usually try to settle conflicts through personal relationships. In addition, some empirical studies have shown that the Chinese tend to have less trust in their legal system because it is considered grafted on and too abstract. Instead, in traditional China, people trusted social norms and rules more. In addition, in ancient China there were effective instruments for successful conflict management through the mutual trust and obligation structures of the *guanxi* networks and the social requirement to protect one's reputation. The need to develop a Chinese legal system based on the model of Western societies only arose through the developmental requirements of modernization processes in Chinese society. A functioning legal system for interactions between Chinese and non-Chinese seems to be becoming indispensable for modern Chinese society.

There were numerous negative assessments of the Chinese legal system from European executives. The ambiguities recognized in this system are often suspected to be sources of feared disadvantages for foreign parties of a conflict. At this point, one can at best speculate as to whether and to what extent these fears of European executives are justified. Either way, this result draws attention to cultural stereotypes and the need to consider them carefully. In concrete conflict cases, it can and should also be a matter for foreign parties to take advantage of the flexibility of the Chinese legal system. The support of Chinese lawyers is indispensable in this context. In addition, it may be helpful for Europeans in China to reach agreements through mediation that help to overcome a conflict before it escalates to the level of a legal dispute.

The results of this research underline the importance of trust for the success of international joint ventures with Chinese companies. An interest in and a great deal

---

4 See Chapter 3.

of respect for the culture of China proves to be an essential building block for developing and maintaining trust. The acquisition of Chinese language skills and knowledge of everyday manners and politeness can communicate this interest, communicating respect, and building mutual trust with Chinese business partners. At the same time, Chinese language skills facilitate access to Chinese culture. The knowledge of cultural differences can also be deepened through intercultural training beyond the education that can be acquired through school, university education, travel and the study of literature. Such training has often proven to be effective. Given its importance, it is all the more surprising that interpersonal trust is obviously not part of the content of intercultural training, as a study by Ehnert (2004) has shown.

Finally, the question arises as to what significance joint ventures will have in Chinese– European economic cooperation going forward. Our respondents have been divided on this issue. In our opinion, if there are major cultural differences and a lack of market knowledge, it is advisable to look for a partner company from the target country with appropriately educated and skillful employees – and therefore the arrangement of joint ventures in China business is also recommended in the future. This form of cooperation accelerates market entry and reduces the entrepreneurial risks of entering a new market for a company. Choosing the right joint venture partner is important. Especially in the research and development (R&D) area, the establishment of joint ventures with Chinese companies should be attractive for European players as well as for the Chinese participants in the coming years. But credibility and continuing trust must be earned!

入乡随俗

as a Chinese proverb says. Loosely translated this means:
When in Rome, do as the Romans do.

8 Conclusion

Although there are numerous studies on German–Chinese economic cooperation between companies, one key success factor has been neglected so far: mutual trust. In view of the different cultural orientations and different economic structures in both countries, managers of German–Chinese joint ventures are particularly challenged when it comes to establishing and sustaining mutual trust. To understand this process better we interviewed German and Chinese executives and content analyzed their statements to reveal the practical dynamics of trust-building and trust-sustaining in on-going German–Chinese joint ventures.

The statements of the managers indicate that there appears to be an asymmetry in mutual trust between German and Chinese executives. The German executives surveyed rate the benevolence and integrity of their Chinese colleagues as rather low, while the majority of Chinese executives commented positively on these dimensions of trust. Regarding the skills attributed to colleagues from other cultures, these executives come to rather positive assessments – albeit with a view to their respectively different skills. These differences in mutual trusting become more comprehensible when the cultural backgrounds of the executives and the conditions of economic cooperation are taken into account. In particular, the social rules prevailing in the two cultures and the culture-specific social categorizations are likely to lead to the trust asymmetries and to the generally rather low level of mutual trust.

For the last twenty years, a great readiness of German and Chinese companies to invest in the other country could be observed. Many German companies report considerable investment intentions for the next few years. Our results identify unfavorable conditions for these investment activities. In the future, it will be necessary to better prepare managers for the cultural differences between Germany and China. Exercising this due diligence may improve the conditions for building mutual trust in German–Chinese joint ventures right now and in the future.

三思而后行

Think three times before you move.

https://doi.org/10.1515/9783111344560-008

Bibliography

Arrow, K. (1972). Gifts and exchanges. *Philosophy and Public Affairs*, **1** (4), 343–362.

Aulakh, P.S., Kotabe, M. & Sahay, A. (1996). Trust and performance in cross-border marketing partnerships: A behavioral approach. *Journal of International Business Studies*, **27** (5), 1005–1032.

Bartelt, A. (2002). *Vertrauen in Zuliefernetzwerken. Eine theoretische und empirische Analyse am Beispiel der Automobilindustrie.* Dissertation, Universität Würzburg. Wiesbaden: Gabler.

Bass, B.M. (1981). *Stogdill's handbook of leadership. A survey of theory and research.* 2nd ed. New York: Free Press.

Bauer, E. (2009). *Internationale Marketingforschung.* 4. Aufl. München: Oldenbourg.

Beamish, P.W. & Banks, J.C. (1987). Equity joint venture and the theory of the multinational enterprise. *Journal International Business Studies*, **18** (2), 1–16.

Bierbrauer, G. (1992). Reactions to violation of normative standards: A cross-cultural analysis of shame and guilt. *International Journal of Psychology*, **27** (2), 181–193.

Blake, R.R. & Mouton, J.S. (1992). *Verhaltenspsychologie im Betrieb. Der Schlüssel zur Spitzenleistung.* Düsseldorf/Wien: ECON Verlag.

Bleicher, K. & Hermann, R. (1991). *Joint–Venture–Management: Erweiterung des eigenen strategischen Aktionsradius.* Stuttgart: Schäffer.

Boersma, M.F., Buckley, P.J. & Ghauri, P.N. (2003). Trust in international joint venture relationships. *Journal of Business Research*, **56**, 1031–1042.

Bond, M.H. (1986). *The psychology of the Chinese people.* Hong Kong: Oxford University Press.

Bond, M.H. (1988). Finding universal dimensions of individual variation in multicultural studies of values: The Rokeach and Chinese Value Surveys. *Journal of Personality and Social Psychology*, **55** (6), 1009–1015.

Bond, M.H. (1991). *Beyond the Chinese face: Insights from psychology.* Hong Kong: Oxford University Press.

Bond, M. H. (1996). Chinese values. In: M.H. Bond (ed.), *The handbook of Chinese psychology* (pp. 208–226). Hong Kong: Oxford University Press.

Bond, M.H. & King, A.Y.C. (1985). Coping with the threat of Westernization in Hong Kong. *International Journal of Intercultural Relations*, **9**, 351–364.

Bornschier, V. (2005). *Culture and politics in economic development.* London: Routledge.

Brahm, L.J. (1995). *Negotiating in China.* Singapore: Reed Academic Publishing Asia.

Branigan, T. (2023). *Red memory. The afterlives of China's cultural revolution.* New York: W.W. Norton.

Brewer, M.B. (1981). Ethnocentrism and its role in interpersonal trust. In: M.B. Brewer & B.E. Collins (eds.), *Scientific inquiry and the social sciences* (pp. 345–359). New York: Jossey- Bass.

Brewer, M.B. (1996). In-group favoritism: The subtle side of intergroup discrimination. In: D.M. Messick & A. Tenbrunsel (eds.), *Codes of conduct: Behavioral research and business ethics* (pp. 160–171). New York: Russell Sage Foundation.

Brodbeck, K.-H. (2010). Grundlagen der buddhistischen Wirtschaftsethik. *Forum Wirtschaftsethik*, **18**, 1, 40–47.

Bromiley, P. & Cummings, L.L. (1995). Transaction costs in organizations with trust. In: R.J. Bies, R.J. Lewicki & B.H. Sheppard (eds.), *Research on negotiation in organizations, vol. 5* (S. 219–247). Bingley, UK: Emerald/JAI Press.

Büchel, B., Prange, C., Probst G. & Rüling, C.-C. (1997). *Joint Venture–Management.* Bern: Paul Haupt.

Bueechl, J., Pudelko, M. & Gillespie, N. (2023). Do Chinese subordinates trust their German supervisors? A model of inter-cultural trust development. *Journal of International Business Studies*, 54 (5), 768–796

Busch, B., Mattes, J. & Sultan, S. (2023). *Zur Abhängigkeit einzelner Industriezweige von China. Eine empirische Bestandsaufnahme.* IW-Report 5/2023. Köln: Institut der deutschen Wirtschaft.

Butek, M., Hildebrandt, J., Klose, M. & Depoux, D. (2023). *The new China story. Short-term instability, long-term strength.* Beijing: China German Chamber of Commerce (GCC).

Cheetham, E. (1994). *Fundamentals of Mainstream Buddhism.* Boston: Charles E. Tuttle Co.

https://doi.org/10.1515/9783111344560-009

Chen, C. & Lee, Y. (2008). *Leadership and management in China: Philosophies, theories, and practices*. Cambridge: Cambridge University Press.

Chen, K.K.S. (1964). *Buddhism in China: A historical survey*. New Jersey: Princeton University Press.

Chen, S. (n.d.). *Aufzeichnungen der drei Königreiche*. https://ctext.org/text.pl?node=604517&if=gb&remap= gb, accessed March 15, 2023.

Cheng, A. (2022). *Grundriss: Geschichte des chinesischen Denkens*. Hamburg: Felix Meiner Verlag.

Child, J., Faulkner, D. & Tallman, S. (2005). *Cooperative strategy: Managing alliances, networks, and joint ventures*. Oxford, UK: Oxford University Press.

China Statistical Yearbook, 2015–2020 editions; National Bureau of Statistics of China, Beijing. http://www. stats.gov.cn/english/Statisticaldata/yearbook/, accessed September 18, 2023.

Chinese Culture Connection (1987). Chinese values and the search for culture-free dimensions of culture. *Journal of Cross-Cultural Psychology*, **18**, 143–164.

Chung, T.Z. & Sievert, H.-W. (1995). *Joint Ventures im chinesischen Kulturkreis. Eintrittsbarrieren überwinden, Marktchancen nutzen*. Wiesbaden: Gabler.

Clases, C., Bachmann, R. & Wehner, T. (2004). Studying trust in virtual organizations. *International Studies of Management & Organization*, **33** (3), 7–27

Clissold, T. (2014). *Chinese rules*. London: William Collins Books.

Collins Dictionary (2023). www.collinsdictionary.com/dictionary/english/, accessed October 26, 2023.

Currall, S.C. & Inkpen, A.C. (2002). A multilevel approach to trust in joint ventures. *Journal of International Business Studies*, **33** (3), 479–495.

Currall, S.C. & Judge, T. (1995). Measuring trust between organizational boundary role persons. *Organizational Behavior and Human Decision Processes*, **64** (2), 151–170.

Cuypers, I.R.P, Ertug, G., Heugens, P.P.M.A.R., Kogut, B. & Zou, T. (2018). The making of a construct: Lessons from 30 years of the Kogut and Singh cultural distance index. *Journal of International Business Studies*, **49** (9), 1138–1153.

Darga, M. (2003). *Laotse*. Kreuzlingen: Hugendubel.

Davis, J.H., Schoorman, F.D., Mayer, R.C. & Tan, H.H. (2000). The trusted general manager and unit performance: Empirical evidence of a competitive advantage. *Strategic Management Journal*, **21** (5), 563–576.

DeBurca, S., Fletcher, R. & Brown, L. (2004). *International marketing. An SME perspective*. Harlow: Prentice-Hall.

Delhey, J., Newton, K. & Welzel, C. (2011). How general is trust in "most people"? Solving the radius of trust problem and deriving a better measure. *American Sociological Review*, **76** (5), 786–807.

Demangeat, J. & Molz, M. (2003): Frankreich. In: A. Thomas (Hrsg.), *Handbuch interkulturelle Kommunikation und Kooperation, Teil 2: Länder, Kulturen und interkulturelle Berufstätigkeit* (pp. 24–52). Göttingen: Vandenhoeck & Ruprecht.

DeSteno, D. (2014). *The truth about trust*. New York: Hudson Street Press/Penguin Random House.

Dimovski, V., Penger, S., Peterlin J. & Uhan, M. (2013). Entrepreneurial leadership in the Daoist framework. *Journal of Enterprising Culture*, **4**, 383–419.

Dirks, K.T. (2000). Trust in leadership and team performance: Evidence from NCAA basketball. *Journal of Applied Psychology*, **85** (6), 1004–1012.

Dirks, K.T. & Ferrin, D.L. (2001). The role of trust in organizational settings. *Organization Science*, **12** (4), 450–467.

Do-Dinh, P. (1987). *Konfuzius*. Hamburg: Rowohlt.

Doney, P.M., Cannon, J.P. & Mullen, M.R. (1998). Understanding the influence of national culture on the development of trust. *Academy of Management Review*, **23** (3), 601–620.

Dong, C. (2005). Zhong Xi shehui xinren de zhidu bijiao (The Western and the Chinese trust concept in comparison). *Study and Exploration*, **156** (1), 114–117.

Döring, N. & Bortz, J. (2016). *Forschungsmethoden und Evaluation in den Sozial- und Humanwissenschaften*. 5. Aufl. Berlin: Springer.

Dostert, E., Fromm, T., Kunkel, C. & Müller, F. (2023). *Risiko? Bereit!* Süddeutsche Zeitung Nr. 143, June 24, 2023, p. 23.

Dowell, D., Morrison, M. & Heffernan, T. (2015). The changing importance of affective trust and cognitive trust across the relationship lifecycle: A study of business-to-business relationships. *Industrial Marketing Management*, **44**, 119–130.

Dürr, N., Rammer, C. & Böing, P. (2020). *Direktinvestitionen zwischen Deutschland und China aus einer innovationspolitischen Sicht*. Studien zum deutschen Innovationssystem, Nr. 8-2020. Berlin: Expertenkommission Forschung und Innovation im Stifterverband für die deutsche Wissenschaft. Zugl. Mannheim: ZEW – Leibniz-Zentrum für Europäische Wirtschaftsforschung.

Earley, C.P. (2006). Leading culture research in the future. A matter of paradigms and taste. *Journal of International Business Studies*, **37** (6), 922–931.

Eggs, H. (2001). *Vertrauen im Electronic Commerce. Herausforderungen und Lösungsansätze*. Wiesbaden: Springer.

Ehnert, I. (2004). *Die Effektivität von interkulturellen Trainings. Überblick über den aktuellen Forschungsstand*. Hamburg. Verlag Dr. Kovač.

Eisele, J. (1995). *Erfolgsfaktoren des Joint-Venture-Management*. Wiesbaden: Gabler.

Elverskog, J. (2006). *Our great Qing. The Mongols, Buddhism and the state in late Imperial China*. Honolulu: University of Hawai'i Press.

Essler, W.K. & Mamat, U. (2006). *Die Philosophie des Buddhismus*. Darmstadt: Wissenschaftliche Buchgesellschaft.

Fan, Y. (2000). A classification of Chinese culture. *Cross Cultural Management: An International Journal*, **7** (2), 3–14.

Fang, T. (1999). *Chinese business negotiating style*. Thousand Oaks, CA.: Sage.

Fargel, M. (2014) Chinesische Jugend aus Sicht der Sozial- und Marktforschung. www.marktforschung.de/dossiers/marktforschung-international/marktforschung-in-china/marktforschung/chinesische-jugend-aus-sicht-der-sozial-und-marktforschung/, accessed October 6, 2021.

Fischer, H.R., Stahl, H.K., Schettgen, D.P. & Schlipat, H. (2019). *Dienende Führung*. Berlin: Erich Schmidt.

Fischer, R. (2012). Chinese work behaviour in a global perspective. In: X. Huang & M.H. Bond (eds.), *Handbook of Chinese organizational behavior: Integrating theory, research and practice* (pp. 48–62). Cheltenham, UK: Edward Elgar.

Flick, U., Kadoff, E. v. & Steinke, I. (2015). *Qualitative Forschung. Ein Handbuch*. 11. Aufl. Reinbek: Rowohlt.

Gao, Y. & Yang, Z. (2006). Zhong Xi shehui xinren jiegou zhi bijiao (A comparison of Western and Chinese trust structures). *Hebei Academic Journal*, **26** (4), 43–48.

Gesk, G. (2020). Das Chinesische Social Credit System—neue Formen der E-Governance zwischen Recht und Policy? In: E. Schwaighofer, F. Kummer & A. Saarenpää (eds.), *IRIS 2020—Verantwortungsbewußte Digitalisierung* (pp. 413–418). Bern: Editions Weblaw.

Gewiss, T. & Oestersporkmann, J. (2017). Key success factors of international joint ventures operating in China—A Sino-German perspective. *Advances in Economics, Business and Management Research*, **37**, 852–866.

Giddens, A. (1999). *Konsequenzen der Moderne*. 3. Aufl. Frankfurt/M.: Suhrkamp.

Gilbert, D.U. (2010). Entwicklungslinien der ökonomischen Vertrauensforschung. In: M. Maring (Hrsg), *Vertrauen – zwischen sozialem Kitt und der Senkung von Transaktionskosten* (pp. 169–197). Karlsruhe: Universitätsverlag—KIT Scientific Publishing.

GLOBE (2021a). https://globeproject.com/results/countries/DEU?menu=list#list, accessed November 23, 2021.

GLOBE (2021b). https://globeproject.com/results/countries/CHN?menu=list#list, accessed November 23, 2021.

Goethe, J.W. v. (2013). *West-östlicher Divan*. Berlin: Holzinger.

Grube, W. (1910). *Religion und Kultus der Chinesen*. Leipzig: Verlag Rudolf Haupt.

Gudykunst, W.B., Ting-Toomey, S. & Chua, E. (1988). *Culture and interpersonal communication*. Newbury Park, CA: Sage.

Guo, Z. (2005). Wenhua: Renwei de chengxu he weiren de quixiang (Culture: Procedure created by human and orientation pursued for human). *Journal of Renmin University of China*, **4**, 24–31.

Gurtman, M.B. (1992). Trust, distrust, and interpersonal problems: A circumplex analysis. *Journal of Personality and Social Psychology*, **62** (6), 989–1002.

Hall, E.T. (1976). *Beyond culture*. Garden City, NY: Anchor Books.

Hall, E.T. (1981). *The silent language*. New York: Anchor Books/Doubleday.

Hall, E.T. (1983). *The dance of life: The other dimension of time*. New York: Anchor Books/Doubleday.

Hall, E.T. & Hall. M.R. (1990). *Understanding cultural differences*. Yarmouth, ME: Intercultural Press.

Hampden-Turner, C. & Trompenaars, A. (1993). *The seven cultures of capitalism*. New York: Currency Doubleday.

Hampden-Turner, C.M. & Trompenaars, F. (1996). A world turned upside down: Doing business in Asia. In: P. Joynt & M. Warner (eds.), *Managing across cultures: Issues and perspectives* (pp. 275–305). London: International Thomson Business Press.

Hansen, C. (1983). *Language and logic in ancient China*. Ann Arbor: University of Michigan Press.

Hansen, K.P. (2000). *Kultur und Kulturwissenschaft. Eine Einführung*. 2. Aufl. Tübingen: Francke.

Hardin, R. (2002). *Trust and trustworthiness*. New York: Russell Sage Foundation.

Hartmann, M. (2020). *Vertrauen. Die unsichtbare Macht*. Frankfurt/M.: S. Fischer Verlag.

Herskovits, M.J. (1948). *Man and his works: The science of cultural anthropology*. New York: A.A. Knopf.

Hildebrandt, J., Butek, M. & Klose, M. (2022). *Rocky roads ahead. Business Confidence Survey 2022/23*. Beijing: China German Chamber of Commerce (GCC).

Hofstede, G. (1980). *Culture's consequences*: International differences in work related values. Beverly Hills, CA: Sage.

Hofstede, G. (1983). National cultures in four dimensions. *International Studies of Management and Organizations*, **13** (1–2), 46–74.

Hofstede, G. (1996). Riding the waves of commerce: A test of Trompenaars' "model" of national culture differences. *International Journal of Intercultural Relations*, **20** (2), 189–198.

Hofstede, G. (2001). *Culture's consequences*: Comparing values, behaviors, institutions and organizations across nations. Thousand Oaks, CA: Sage.

Hofstede, G. (2006). What did GLOBE really measure? Researchers' minds versus respondents' minds. *Journal of International Business Studies*, **37** (6), 882–896.

Hofstede, G. & Bond, M.H. (1988). The Confucius connection. From cultural roots to economic growth. *Organizational Dynamics*, **14** (4), 4–21.

Hofstede, G., Hofstede, G.J. & Minkov, M. (2010). *Cultures and organizations: Software of the mind*. 3rd ed. New York: McGraw-Hill.

Hong, J. & Shouxiang, W. (2009). *Kulturbegriff aus Sicht der Chinesen*. Presentation given at the University of Science and Technology of China, Hefei.

Hornung, F. (2013). *Instabilität internationaler Joint Ventures: Eine theoriebasierte, empirische Untersuchung am Beispiel deutsch-internationaler Joint Ventures*. Diss. Gießen: Justus-Liebig Universität.

House, R.J., Hanges, P.J., Ruiz-Quintanilla, S.A., Dorfman, P.W., Javidan, M., Dickson, M. & Gupta, V. (2004). *Culture, leadership and organizations. The GLOBE study of 62 societies*. 3rd ed. Thousand Oaks, CA: Sage.

House, R.J. & Javidan, M. (2004). Overview of GLOBE. In: R.J. House, P.J. Hanges, M. Javidan, P.W. Dorfman & V. Gupta (eds.), *Culture, leadership, and organizations. The GLOBE study of 62 societies* (S. 9–28). Thousand Oaks, CA: Sage.

Huff, L. & Kelley, L. (2003). Levels of organizational trust in individualist versus collectivist societies: A seven-nation study. *Organization Science*, **14** (1), 81–90.

Inglehart, R. (1998). *Modernisierung und Postmodernisierung. Kultureller, wirtschaftlicher und politischer Wandel in 43 Gesellschaften*. Frankfurt/M.: Campus.

Jing, Y. & Bond, M.H. (2015). Sources for trusting most people: How national goals for socializing children promote the contributions made by trust of the in-group and the out-group to non-specific trust. *Journal of Cross-Cultural Psychology*, **46** (2), 191–210.

Johnson, J.L., Cullen, J.B., Sakano, T. & Takenouchi, H. (1996). Setting the stage for trust and strategic integration in Japanese–U.S. cooperative alliances. *Journal of International Business Studies*, **27** (5), 981–1004.

Jullien, F. (1999). *Über das Fade: Eine Eloge zu Denken und Ästhetik in China*. Berlin: Merve.

Kale, P., Singh, H. & Perlmutter, H. (2000). Learning and protection of proprietary assets in strategic alliances: Building relational capital. *Strategic Management Journal*, **21** (3), 217–237.

Kalinke, V. (2011). *Nichtstun als Handlungsmaxime: Studien zu Laozi Daodejing, Bd. 3: Essay zur Rationalität des Mystischen*. Leipzig: Leipziger Literaturverlag.

Kalinke, V. (2015). *Studien zu Laozi, Daodejing, Bd. 1: Eine Wiedergabe seines Deutungsspektrums: Text, Übersetzung, Zeichenlexikon und Konkordanz*. 2. Aufl. Leipzig: Leipziger Literaturverlag.

Kalinke, V. (2019). *Zhuangzi. Das Buch der daoistischen Weisheit. Gesamttext*. Ditzingen: Reclam.

Kam, C.S.C. & Bond, M.H. (2009). Emotional reactions of anger and shame to the norm violation characterizing episodes of interpersonal harm. *British Journal of Social Psychology*, **48**, 203–219.

King, A.Y.C. & Bond, M.H. (1985). The Confucian paradigm of man. In W.S. Tseng & D.Y.H. Wu (eds.), *Chinese culture and mental health: An overview* (pp. 29–45). Orlando, FL: Academic Press.

Kogut, B. & Singh, H. (1988). The effect of national culture on the choice of entry mode. *Journal of International Business Studies*, **19** (3), 411–432.

Kohn, L. (2004). *Daoism and Chinese Culture*. Cambridge: Three Pines Press.

Koller, M. (1988). Risk as a determinant of trust. *Basic and Applied Social Psychology*, **9** (4), 265–276.

Konara, P. & Mohr, A. (2019). Why we should stop using the Kogut and Singh index. *Management International Review*, **59** (3), 335–354.

Kong, X. & Legge, J. (2009). *The analects of Confucius*. Beijing: Foreign Language Press.

Kotabe, M. & Helsen, K. (2001). *Global marketing management*. 2nd ed. Hoboken, NJ: John Wiley & Sons.

Kowal, S. & O'Connell, D. (2003). Zur Transkription von Gesprächen. In: U. Flick, E. von Kardoff & I. Steinke (eds.), *Qualitative Forschung: Ein Handbuch* (pp. 436–446). Reinbek: Rowohlt.

Kramer, R.M. (1999). Trust and distrust in organizations: Emerging perspectives, enduring questions. *Annual Review of Psychology*, **50**, 569–598.

Krause, C. (2018). Auf Spurensuche 1978–2018: Zur Entwicklung des chinesischen Buddhismus in der Gegenwart. *China heute*, **XXXVII**, 3 (199), 176–188.

Krishnan, R., Martin, X., & Noorderhaven, N.G. (2006). When does trust matter to alliance performance? *Academy of Management Journal*, **49** (5), 894–917.

Kriz, A. & Keating, B. (2010). Business relationships in China: Lessons about deep trust. *Asia Pacific Business Review*, **16** (3), 299–318.

Kruse, J. (2006). *Einführung in die qualitative Interviewforschung*. Freiburg: FB Soziologie der Universität Freiburg.

Küng, H. (1992). *Projekt Weltethos*. 12. Aufl. München: Piper.

Küng, H. & Ching, J. (1988). *Christentum und Chinesische Religion*. München: Piper.

Kuhn, T.S. (1970). *The structure of scientific revolutions*. 2nd ed. Chicago: University of Chicago Press.

Laenderdaten.info (n. d.). Verbreitung des Buddhismus. www.laenderdaten.info/religionen/buddhismus.php, accessed February 20, 2023.

Lamnek, S. & Krell, C. (2016). *Qualitative Sozialforschung*. 6. Aufl. Weinheim: Beltz.

Lane, C. (1998). Introduction: Theories and issues in the study of trust. In: C. Lane & R. Bachmann (eds.), *Trust within and between organizations. Conceptual issues and empirical applications* (pp. 1–30). New York: Oxford University Press.

Lang, N.S. (1998). *Intercultural management in China: Strategies of Sino-European and Sino-Japanese joint ventures*. Wiesbaden: Deutscher Universitätsverlag.

Larson, A. (1992). Network dyads in entrepreneurial settings: A study of the governance of exchange relationships. *Administrative Science Quarterly*, **37**, 76–104.

Leung, K. (2012). Theorizing about Chinese organizational behavior. In X. Huang & M.H. Bond (eds.), *Handbook of Chinese organizational behavior: Integrating theory, research and practice* (pp. 13–28). Cheltenham, UK: Edward Elgar.

Lewicki, R.J. & Bunker, B.B. (1995). Trust in relationships: A model of trust development and decline. In: B.B. Bunker & J.Z. Rubin (eds.), *Conflict, cooperation, and justice* (pp. 133–173). San Francisco: Jossey-Bass.

Lewis, J.D. & Weigert, A.J. (1985). Trust as a social reality. *Social Forces*, **63**, 967–985.

Li, H. (1977). *China's political situation and the power struggle in Peking*. Hong Kong: Lung Men Press.

Li, S.Z. (1994). Quanqiuhua yu zhongguo wenhua (Globalisierung und chinesische Kultur). In: *Zhongguo wenhua chuantong yu xiandaihua (Chinesische Kulturtradition und Modernisierung)* (pp. 3–12). Beijing: Zhongguo shuju.

Lin, B. & Li, P. (2005). Bijiao shiyu zhong de Zhong Xi xinrenguan (Chinese and Western perspectives on trust in comparison). *Journal of Sun Yat-sen University (Social Science Edition)*, **45** (3), 101–107.

Linggi, D. (2011). *Vertrauen in China. Ein kritischer Beitrag zur kulturvergleichenden Sozialforschung*. Wiesbaden: VS Verlag.

Locke, K.D. (2001). *Grounded theory in management research*. London: Sage.

Louis, F. (2003). The genesis of an icon: The "taiji" diagram´s early history. *Harvard Journal of Asiatic Studies*, **63** (1), 145–196.

Luhmann, N. (2014). *Vertrauen. Ein Mechanismus zur Reduktion sozialer Komplexität*. 5. Aufl. Konstanz: UVK.

Luo, Y. (2001). Antecedents and consequences of personal attachment in cross-cultural cooperative ventures. *Administrative Science Quarterly*, **46** (2), 177–201.

Madhok, A. (1995). *Opportunism and trust in joint venture relationships: An exploratory study and a model*. Diss. University of Utah, Salt Lake City.

Markowsky, R. & Thomas, A. (1995). *Studienhalber in Deutschland. Interkulturelles Orientierungstraining für amerikanische Studenten, Schüler und Praktikanten*. Heidelberg: Asanger.

Maseland, R. & van Hoorn, A. (2009). Explaining the negative correlation between values and practices. A note on the Hofstede–GLOBE Debate. *Journal of International Business Studies*, **40** (3), 527–532.

Mauritz, H. (1996). *Interkulturelle Geschäftsbeziehungen*. Wiesbaden: Deutscher Universitätsverlag.

Mayer, R.C. & Davis, J.H. (1999). The effect of the performance appraisal system on trust for management: A field quasi-experiment. *Journal of Applied Psychology*, **84** (1), 123–136.

Mayer, R.C., Davis, J.H. & Schoorman, F.D. (1995). An integrative model of organizational trust. *Academy of Management Review*, **20** (3), 709–734.

Mayring, P.A.E. (2002). *Einführung in die qualitative Sozialforschung*. 5. Aufl. Weinheim: Beltz.

McClelland, D.C. (1966). *Die Leistungsgesellschaft. Psychologische Analyse der Voraussetzungen wirtschaftlicher Entwicklung*. Stuttgart: Kohlhammer.

McEvily, B. & Tortoriello, M. (2011). Measuring trust in organisational research: Review and recommendations. *Journal of Trust Research*, **1** (1), 23–63.

McKnight, D.H., Cummings, L. & Chervany, N.L. (1998). Initial trust formation in new organizational relationships. *Academy of Management Review*, **23** (3), 473–490.

Mead, R. & Andrews, T.G. (2009). *International management—culture and beyond*. 4th ed. Chichester: Wiley.

Meyerson, D., Weick, K. & Kramer, R.M. (1996). Swift trust and temporary groups. In: R.M. Kramer & T. Tyler (eds.), *Trust in organizations* (pp. 166–195). Thousand Oaks, CA: Sage.

Minkov, M. (2007). *What makes us different and similar: A new interpretation of the World Values Survey and other cross-cultural data*. Sofia, BG: Klasika i Stil.

Minkov, M. (2011). *Cultural differences in a globalizing world*. Bingley, UK: Emerald.

Minkov, M. & Kaasa, A. (2022). Do dimensions of culture exist objectively? A validation of the revised Minkov–Hofstede model of culture with World Values Survey items and scores for 102 countries. *Journal of International Management*, **28** (4), 100971.

Morden, T. (1999). Models of national culture—a management review. *Cross Cultural Management*, **6** (1), 19–44.

Morrow Jr., J.L., Hansen, M.H. & Pearson, A.W. (2004). The cognitive and affective antecedents of general trust within cooperative organizations. *Journal of Managerial Issues*, **16** (1), 48–64.

Müller, S. & Gelbrich, K. (2015). *Interkulturelles Marketing*. 2. Aufl. München: Vahlen.

Muethel, M. & Bond, M.H. (2013). National context and individual employees' trust of the out-group: The role of societal trust. *Journal of International Business Studies*, **44**, 312–333.

Ng, P.W.-K., Lau, C.-M. & Nyaw, M.-K. (2007). The effect of trust on international joint venture performance in China. *Journal of International Management*, **13**, 430–448.

Nippa M. & Reuer, J.J. (2019). On the future of international joint venture research. *Journal of International Business Studies*, **50**, 555–597.

Nisbett, R.E., Peng, K., Choi, I. & Norenzayan, A. (2001). Culture and systems of thought: Holistic versus analytic cognition. *Psychological Review*, **108** (2), 291–310.

Nooteboom, B., Berger, H. & Noorderhaven, N.G. (1997). Effects of trust and governance on relational risk. *Academy of Management Journal*, **40** (2), 308–338.

Nyanatiloka (2007). *Das Wort des Buddha*. Stammbach-Herrnschrot: Verlag Beyerlein & Steinschulte.

Okazaki, S. & Mueller, B. (2007). Cross-cultural advertising research. Where we have been and where we need to go. *International Marketing Review*, **24** (5), 499–518.

Oldham, G. (1975). The impact of supervisory characteristics on goal acceptance. *Academy of Management Journal*, **18** (3), 461–475.

Parkhe, A. (1993). Partner nationality and the structure–performance relationship in strategic alliances. *Organization Science*, **4**, 301–314.

Payne, R. & Clark, M. (2003). Dispositional and situational determinants of trust in two types of managers. *The International Journal of Human Resource Management*, **14** (1), 128–138.

Peill-Schoeller, P. (1994). *Interkulturelles Management: Synergien in Joint Ventures zwischen China und deutschsprachigen Ländern*. Heidelberg: Springer.

Peng, K., Spencer-Rodgers, J. & Zhong, N. (2006). Naïve dialecticism and the Tao of Chinese thought. In U. Kim, K.-S. Yang, & K.-K. Hwang (eds.), *Indigenous and cultural psychology: Understanding people in context* (pp. 247–262). New York: Springer.

Perlitz, M. & Schrank, R. (2013). *Internationales Management*. 6. Aufl. Konstanz: UVK.

Rich, G. (1997). The sales manager as a role model: Effects on trust, job satisfaction and performance of salespeople. *Journal of the Academy of Marketing Science*, **25**, 319–328.

Ring, P.S. & van de Ven, A.H. (1994). Developmental processes of co-operative inter- organizational relationships. *Academy of Management Review*, **19** (1), 90–118.

Roetz, H. (1995). *Konfuzius*. München: C.H. Beck.

Rohm, M. (2017). *Modelling critical success factors of international joint ventures in real estate development: Perspective of a capital investor*. Diss. Cheltenham: University of Gloucestershire.

Rotter, J.B. (1967). A new scale for the measurement of interpersonal trust. *Journal of Personality*, **35** (4), 651–665.

Rousseau, D.M., Sitkin, S.B., Burt, R.S. & Camerer, C. (1998). Not so different after all: A cross-discipline view of trust. *Academy of Management Review*, **23** (3), 393–404.

Rubin, H.J. & Rubin, I.S. (2012). *Qualitative interviewing. The art of hearing data*. 3rd ed. Los Angeles, CA: Sage.

Saldana, J. (2009). *The coding manual for qualitative researchers*. Los Angeles, CA: Sage.

Salomon, E. (2008). *Hybrides Management in sino-österreichischen Joint Ventures in China aus österreichischer Perspektive*. Diss. Wien: Wirtschaftsuniversität.

Schäfers, B. et al. (Hrsg.) (2003). *Grundbegriffe der Soziologie*. Heidelberg: Springer.

Scharmann T. & Roth, E. (1976). *Vom Proletarier zum Industriebürger*. Bern: Hans Huber.

Schein, E.H. (1992). *Organizational culture and leadership*. 2nd ed. San Francisco: Jossey- Bass.

Schipper, K., Girardot, N. & Duval, K.C. (1993). *The Taoist body*. Oakland, CA: University of California Press.

Schluchter, W. (1983). *Max Webers Studien über Konfuzianismus und Taoismus*. Frankfurt/M.: Suhrkamp.

Schmidt-Glintzer, H. (2005). *Der Buddhismus*. München: C.H. Beck.

Schmidt-Glintzer, H. (2008). *Kleine Geschichte Chinas*. München: C.H. Beck.

Schmidt-Glintzer, H. (2020). *Das neue China: Vom Untergang des Kaiserreichs bis zur Gegenwart*. 7. Aufl. München: C.H. Beck.

Schneider, U. (1997). *Der Buddhismus: Eine Einführung*. 4. Aufl. Darmstadt: Wissenschaftliche Buchgesellschaft.

Schoorman, F.D., Mayer, R.C. & Davis, J.H. (2007). An integrative model of organizational trust: Past, present, and future. *Academy of Management Review, 32* (2), 344–354.

Schroll-Machl, S. (2001). *Businesskontakte zwischen Deutschen und Tschechen. Kulturunterschiede in der Wirtschaftszusammenarbeit*. Sternenfels: Wissenschaft & Praxis.

Schroll-Machl, S. (2003). Deutschland. In: A. Thomas, S. Kammhuber & S. Schroll-Machl (Hrsg.), *Handbuch Interkulturelle Kommunikation und Kooperation, Bd.2: Länder und Kulturen und interkulturelle Berufstätigkeit* (pp. 72–89). Göttingen: Vandenhoeck & Ruprecht.

Schuchardt, C.A. (1994). *Deutsch-chinesische Joint-ventures*. München: Oldenbourg.

Schumann, H.W. (2004). *Der historische Buddha: Leben und Lehre des Gotama*. Kreuzlingen/München: Heinrich Hugendubel Verlag.

Schwartz, S.H. (1992). Universals in the content and structure of values. Theoretical advances and empirical tests in 20 countries. In M.P. Zanna (ed.), *Advances in experimental social psychology*, Vol. 25 (pp. 1–65). San Diego, CA: Academic Press.

Schwartz, S.H. (1994a). Beyond individualism/collectivism: New cultural dimensions of values. In U. Kim, H.C. Triandis, C. Kagitcibasi, S.C. Choi & G. Yoon (eds.), *Individualism and collectivism: Theory, method, and applications* (pp. 85–119). Thousand Oaks, CA: Sage.

Schwartz, S.H. (1994b). Are there universal aspects in the structure and contents of human values? *Journal of Social Issues, 50* (4), 19–45.

Schwartz, S.H. (1999). A theory of cultural values and some implications for work. *Applied Psychology, 48* (1), 23–47.

Schwartz, S.H. (2008). *Cultural value orientations: Nature and implications of national differences*. Working paper, The Hebrew University of Jerusalem.

Schwartz, S.H. & Bilsky, W. (1990). Toward a theory of the universal content and structure of values. Extensions and cross-cultural replications. *Journal of Personality and Social Psychology, 58* (5), 878–891.

Schwartz, S.H. & Huismans, S. (1995). Value priorities and religiosity in four western religions. *Social Psychology Quarterly, 58* (2), 88–107.

Shapiro, S.P. (1987). The social control of impersonal trust. *American Journal of Sociology, 93* (3), 623–658.

Sievert, H.-W. (2005). Netzwerkdenken und Netzwerkhandeln im chinesischen Kontext. In: T. Claus, K. Helling, A. Knaden & M. Kramer (Hrsg.), *Virtuelle Netze – Festschrift für Thomas Witte* (pp. 165–180). Frankfurt/M.: Verlag Peter Lang.

Sievert, H.-W. (2009). Die Kultur Chinas in ihren Auswirkungen auf das Management von deutsch-chinesischen Joint Ventures. In: C. von Bar, H. Hellwege, J.M. Mössner & N. Winkeljohann (Hrsg.), *Recht und Wirtschaft. Gedächtnisschrift für Malte Schindhelm* (pp. 527–548). Köln: Carl Heymanns.

Sievert, H.-W., Klinger, E. & Bierbrauer, G. (2010). *Deutscher Mittelstand im Ausland. Erwartungen und Erfahrungen*. Frankfurt/M.: PricewaterhouseCoopers.

Simon, R. (2009). *Daodejing: Das Buch vom Weg und seiner Wirkung*. Stuttgart: Reclam.

Slingerland, E. & Kleinschmidt, B. (2014). *Das Wu-Wei-Prinzip*. Berlin: Berlin Verlag.

Smith, P.B. (2006). When elephants fight, the grass gets trampled. The GLOBE and Hofstede projects. *Journal of International Business Studies*, **37** (6), 915–921.

Smith, P.B. & Dugan, S. (1996). National culture and the values of organizational employees. *Journal of Cross-Cultural Psychology*, **27** (2), 231–264.

Smith, P.B., Trompenaars, F. & Dugan, S. (1995). The Rotter Locus of Control Scale in 43 countries: A test of cultural relativity. *International Journal of Psychology*, **30** (3), 377–400.

Soares, A.M., Farhangmehr, M. & Shoham, A. (2007). Hofstede's dimensions of culture in international marketing studies. *Journal of Business Research*, **60** (3), 277–284.

Søndergaard, M. (1994). Hofstede's consequences: A study of reviews, citations, and replications. *Organization Studies*, **15** (3), 447–456.

Sorrentino, R.M., Holmes, J.G., Hanna, S.E. & Sharp, A. (1995). Uncertainty orientation and trust in close relationships: Individual differences in cognitive styles. *Journal of Personality and Social Psychology*, **68** (2), 314–327.

Stahl, G.K., Chua, C.H. & Pablo, A.L. (2003). *Trust following acquisitions*: *A three-country comparative study of employee reactions to takeovers*. Academy of Management Best Conference Paper Proceedings, Paper N6.

Stening, B. & Zhang, M. (2007). Methodological challenges confronted when conducting management research in China. *International Journal of Cross-Cultural Management*, **7** (1), 121–142.

Stepan-Meyer, J. (2021). Joint Venture in China: Ein Auslaufmodell oder Kooperationsform der Zukunft? In: T. Loitsch (Hrsg.), *China im Blickpunkt des 21. Jahrhunderts. Impulsgeber für Wirtschaft, Wissenschaft und Gesellschaft* (pp. 205–219). 2. Aufl. Berlin: Springer Gabler.

Strauss, A. & Corbin, J. (1994). Grounded theory methodology: An overview. In: N.K. Denzin & Y.S. Lincoln (eds.), *Handbook of qualitative research* (pp. 273–285). Thousand Oaks, CA: Sage.

Strauss, A. & Corbin, J. (1996). *Grounded Theory*: *Grundlagen qualitativer Sozialforschung*. Weinheim: Beltz.

Tang, Z. & Reisch, B. (1995). *Erfolg im China-Geschäft*. Frankfurt/M.: Campus.

Taylor, R.G. (1989). The role of trust in labor–management relations. *Organization Development Journal*, **7**, 85–89.

Thomas, A. (2003). Kultur und Kulturstandards. In: A. Thomas, S. Kammhuber & S. Schroll- Machl (Hrsg.), *Handbuch Interkulturelle Kommunikation und Kooperation, Bd.1: Grundlagen und Praxisfelder* (pp. 19–31). Göttingen: Vandenhoeck & Ruprecht.

Thomas, A. & Schenk, E. (2001). *Beruflich in China. Trainingsprogramm für Manager, Fach- und Führungskräfte*. Göttingen: Vandenhoeck & Ruprecht.

Thomas, A., Schenk, E. & Heisel, W. (2008). *Beruflich in China. Trainingsprogramm für Manager, Fach- und Führungskräfte*. 3. Aufl. Göttingen: Vandenhoeck & Ruprecht.

Thomas, D.C. & Peterson, M.F. (2018). *Cross-cultural management. Essential concepts*. 4th ed. Los Angeles: Sage.

Tong, C.K. & Yong, P.K. (1998). Guanxi bases, xinyong and Chinese business networks. *The British Journal of Sociology*, **49** (1), 75–96.

Trommsdorff, V. & Wilpert, B. (1994). *Deutsch-Chinesische Joint Ventures: Wirtschaft— Recht—Kultur*. 2. Aufl. Wiesbaden: Gabler.

Trompenaars, A. & Hampden-Turner, C. (1997). *Riding the waves of culture. Understanding cultural diversity in global business*. 2nd ed. London: Irwin.

Trompenaars, F. (1993). *Handbuch globales managen: Wie man kulturelle Unterschiede im Geschäftsleben versteht*. Düsseldorf: ECON.

Tylor, E.B. (1871). *Primitive culture: Researches into the development of mythology, philosophy, religion, art, and custom*. London: John Murray.

Usunier, J.-C. (2000). *Marketing across cultures*. Harlow: Prentice-Hall.

Van Ess, H. (2009). *Der Konfuzianismus*. 2. Aufl. München: C.H. Beck.

Van Ess, H. (2011). *Der Daoismus*: *Von Laozi bis heute*. München: C.H. Beck.

Van Everdingen, Y.M. & Waarts, E. (2003). *A multi-country study of the adoption of ERP systems: The effect of national culture*. ERIM Report Series Research in Management, Report Nr. ERS-2003-019-MKT. Rotterdam: Erasmus Universiteit, Erasmus Research Institute of Management.

Venaik, P. & Brewer, S. (2010). Avoiding uncertainty in Hofstede and GLOBE. *Journal of International Business Studies*, **41** (8), 1294–1315.

Verstappen, S.H. (1999). *The thirty-six strategies of ancient China*. San Francisco: China Books & Periodicals.

Vollmer, P. (2012). Gründungen in China: Joint Venture war gestern. *Wirtschaftswoche*, September 6, 2012.

Von Brück, M. (2016). *Einführung in den Buddhismus*. 4. Aufl. Frankfurt/M.: Verlag der Weltreligionen.

Von Glasenapp, H. (1978). *Der Pfad zur Erleuchtung*. Düsseldorf/Köln: Diederichs.

Von Senger, H. (2000). *Strategeme. Lebens- und Überlebenslisten aus drei Jahrtausenden*. 10. Aufl. Bern: Scherz.

Waley, A.D. (1938). Confucius. The analects of Confucius. London: George Allen & Unwin.

Wang, R.R. (2012). *Yinyang: The way of heaven and earth in Chinese thought and culture*. Cambridge: Cambridge University Press.

Wilhelm, R. (1989). *Kungfutse. Gespräche—Lun Yü*. München: Diederichs.

Williams, M. (2001). In whom we trust: Group membership as an affective context for trust development. *Academy of Management Review*, **26** (3), 377–396.

Willinger, M., Keser, C., Lohmann, C. & Usunier, J.-C. (2003). A comparison of trust and reciprocity between France and Germany: Experimental investigation based on the investment game. *Journal of Economic Psychology*, **24**, 447–466.

Woesler, M. (2010). *Der Konfuzianismus als Hauptströmung der chinesischen Geistesgeschichte. Mit einer zweisprachigen Ausgabe der Lunyu (Gespräche/Analekte) des Konfuzius*. Dülmen: Europäischer Universitätsverlag.

Wrightsman, L.S. (1991). Interpersonal trust and attitudes toward human nature. In J.P. Robinson, P.R. Shaver, & L.S. Wrightsman (eds.), *Measures of social psychological attitudes, Vol. 1. Measures of personality and social psychological attitudes* (pp. 373–412). London, New York: Academic Press.

Wuttke, J. (2012). A practitioner's perspective on organizational behavior in China. In X. Huang & M.H. Bond (eds.), *Handbook of Chinese organizational behavior* (pp. 63–83). Cheltenham, UK: Edward Elgar.

Yamagishi, T. (2011). *Trust: The evolutionary game of mind and society*. Tokyo: Springer.

Yamagishi, T. & Yamagishi, M. (1994). Trust and commitment in the United States and Japan. *Motivation and Emotion*, **18** (2), 129–166.

Yoo, B., Donthu, N. & Lenartowicz, T. (2011). Measuring Hofstede's five dimensions of cultural values at the individual level. Development and validation of CVSCALE. *Journal of International Consumer Marketing*, **23** (3–4), 193–210.

Zaheer, A., McEvily, B. & Perrone, V. (1998). Does trust matter? Exploring the effects of interorganizational and interpersonal trust on performance. *Organization Science*, **9** (2), 141–159.

Zaheer, S. & Zaheer, A. (2006). Trust across borders. *Journal of International Business Studies*, **37**, 21–29.

Zak, P.L. & Knack, S. (2001). Trust and growth. *The Economic Journal*, **111** (470), 295–321.

Zhu, Z. (2006). *zhongguo wenhu jiangyi (Lehrmaterialien der chinesischen Kultur)*. Wuhan: Verlag der Technischen Universität Wuhan.

List of Figures

https://doi.org/10.1515/9783111344560-010

List of Tables

https://doi.org/10.1515/9783111344560-011

About the Authors

Dr. Edgar Klinger is Lecturer in International Management and Marketing at the University of Osnabrück and the Welfenakademie in Braunschweig.

Prof. Dr. Hans-Wolf Sievert can look back on 50 years of experience as an entrepreneur in Chinese business. Furthermore, he is Honorary Professor for Intercultural Management at the University of Tübingen and the University of Osnabrück. He has also taught at Chinese universities as a visiting professor. In 2012, he founded the Sievert Foundation for Science and Culture which initiated this study.

Günter Bierbrauer was Professor of Psychology at the University of Osnabrück, and he was also a permanent Visiting Professor of Legal Psychology at the Law Faculty of the University of Lucerne, Switzerland.

Prof. Michael Harris Bond is Visiting Chair Professor of Management at the Hong Kong Polytechnic University, teaching cross-cultural management. He is the co-editor of *The Handbook of Chinese Organizational Behavior*.

https://doi.org/10.1515/9783111344560-012

Index

https://doi.org/10.1515/9783111344560-013

www.ingramcontent.com/pod-product-compliance
Lightning Source LLC
Chambersburg PA
CBHW061817210326
41599CB00034B/7027